Your One-Stop
Guide to
the Mass

Your One-Stop Guide to the Mass

FR. DALE FUSHEK
and BILL DODDS

CHARIS

SERVANT PUBLICATIONS
ANN ARBOR, MICHIGAN

Charis Books is an imprint of Servant Publications especially designed to serve
Roman Catholics.

Verses marked NRSV are from the Revised Standard Version of the Bible, copy-
righted 1989 by the Division of Christian Education of the National Council of
Churches of Christ in the USA. Used by permission. All rights reserved.

Excerpts from the English translation of the *Catechism of the Catholic Church* for
the United States of America. © 1994, United States Catholic Conference, Inc.-
Libreria Editrice Vaticana. Used with permission.

Excerpts from the English translation of the *Catechism of the Catholic Church:
Modifications from the "Editio Typica."* © 1997, United States Catholic
Conference, Inc.-Libreria Editrice Vaticana. Used with Permission.

Servant Publications
P.O. Box 8617
Ann Arbor, MI 48107

Cover design: Hile Illustration and Design, Ann Arbor, Michigan

    01 02 03 10 9 8 7 6 5 4

Printed in the United States of America
ISBN 1-56955-219-3

LIBRARY OF CONGRESS CATALOGING-IN-PUBLICATION DATA

Dodds, Bill.
Your one-stop guide to the Mass / Bill Dodds and Dale Fushek.
    p.   cm.
Includes index.
ISBN 1-56955-219-3
1. Mass.   I. Fushek, Dale.
BX2230.5.D63   2000
264'.02036—dc21   00-058923

Contents

1. Just What *Is* the Mass ... and What Does It Have to Do With Me? / 7

2. Our Jewish Roots / 19

3. Getting in Shape Over Centuries / 33

4. The Council of Trent: Not Quite Carved in Stone / 49

5. The Words We Pray Show What We Believe / 61

6. The Ultimate—and Perfect—Sacrifice / 85

7. The Liturgical Year: Every Day is Someone's Feast / 101

8. Going Beyond Those Sixty Minutes / 121

9. How to Worship at a Mass that "Fits Right" / 133

Notes / 145

Index / 147

Dedication

For Justin Dale Keough, Timothy Dale Blum,
Michael Dale Junker, Kolbe Dale Poarch,
Anthony Dale Cook and Noah Dale Baniewicz.
–D.F.

For the regulars at daily Mass at St. Pius X Church,
Mountlake Terrace, Washington.
–B.D.

CHAPTER ONE

Just What Is the Mass ... and What Does It Have to Do With Me?

Sunday morning at St. So-and-So's. Mass at 8:30, 10 and 11:45. Kind of like a movie theater, right? Different show times, but the same flick.

And once you've been there/done that, what's the point? How many times can you watch a rerun before it loses all meaning?

So why does the Catholic Church say this is its central form of worship? And, let's be honest here, how can it expect people to keep going to the same thing week after week? Month after month. Year after year.

The "Holy Sacrifice of the Mass" might have been high drama and big-time entertainment for medieval serfs, but *we* have televisions that get more than five hundred channels. Except a church isn't a movie theater. The Mass isn't a film. And what happens during the celebration wasn't meant to be entertainment.

It's more than that. It's an encounter. It's a miracle. It's representing, presenting once again, what happened almost two thousand years ago.

It's an encounter with God—with Christ—in a unique and personal way. An encounter as a community but, at the same time, a meeting that's one-on-one.

It's a miracle. There's no other way to describe it. The *Catechism of the Catholic Church* (*CCC*) puts it like this: "The priest, in the role of Christ, pronounces these words" of consecration "but their power and grace are God's. This is my body, he says. This word transforms the things offered" into Jesus.[1]

Not a *symbol,* in our traditional sense of the word. (*Go to: Q. & A.: "What is 'Transubstantiation'? at the end of this chapter.*)

And it's re-presenting what happened at the first Mass—at the Last Supper—when, on the night before he died, Jesus *instituted* the Eucharist. (We'll talk more about that in chapter 2.) And it's a re-presenting of what happened the next afternoon, Good Friday, when he was put to death. (We'll look at that in chapter 6.)

And it's more. To use a common expression, the Mass is a two-way street. "It is the culmination both of God's action sanctifying the world in Christ and of the worship men [all people] offer to Christ and through him to the Father in the Holy Spirit."[2]

It isn't just God offering all those things to us. It's the best way we can worship the Father, Son and Spirit. The way that ties all the other ways into a nice, neat package of love.

It's by the Mass that "we already unite ourselves with the heavenly liturgy and anticipate eternal life, when God will be all in all" (*CCC* 1326, cf. *1 Cor* 15:28). It is, truly, a little bit of heaven on earth. At Mass, we join with those who have gone before us and are already in heaven and those who have died but are still preparing to enter heaven. We form a single group in prayer. We are a *mystical body* with Christ as our head.

"In brief, the Eucharist is the sum and summary of our faith: 'Our way of thinking is attuned to the Eucharist, and the Eucharist in turn confirms our way of thinking.'"[3] The Mass is the whole story: God entered into human history in a particular way. He sent his Son. His Son died for us and rose from the dead. Because of that, we can look forward to one day being with the Father, Son and Spirit forever. And the Mass, for us now, is like the needle on a compass. It orients our lives.

That's what it is, in theological terms. Does that mean we have to be scholars to begin to grasp its meaning? Its purpose, its beauty, its possibilities?

Thank God, no.

At the Mass, through the Mass, the youngest soul can be enriched by grace, by God's blessing and presence. The hardest heart can begin to soften. The most frightened, troubled or discouraged mind can glimpse hope.

At the same time, we can let Mass become routine. That "rerun." An obligation we grudgingly fulfill. Sixty minutes we endure to keep our parents happy. Or to set an example for our kids. Or to placate our spouse.

We get to decide how we will approach the Mass because we have choice. We have free will. It's a gift from God. He invites and lets us decide. He offers and lets us refuse. He permits that, even as he knows that if we accept his invitation, if we take him up on his offer, we will be better off. It's to our advantage to do those things but we don't have to do them.

Why will we be better off? Is it because we'll become some Holy Joe or Jane, with all the negative connotations attached to those labels? No. Not at all.

We'll be better off because we were created to be with him. Created by Love, we were made to love. To love ourselves, to love others, to love our God. Bottom line, we really are "love machines." And if we don't love, if we refuse love or turn away from opportunities to grow in love and to encounter love, we're malfunctioning. We're setting ourselves up for future troubles.

The One who created us gave us the potential to do that for which we were created. That's worth repeating: The One who created us gave us the potential to do that for which we were created. To love.

And he gave us the free will to use, misuse or ignore that potential.

What's in It for You?

When it comes to the Mass, what's in it for you? Every good gift imaginable and infinitely more beyond imagining. Not an end to troubles and sickness, to pain and death, but the greater realization of an accompanying Presence through them.

The Mass lets you see how the story ends. And it gives you the opportunity to be a part of it, here and now, and in the next life.

At the same time—life is complex, isn't it?—one way we can "get more" out of the Mass is to learn more about it. Nothing magical, mystical or theological about that. The folks who most enjoy watching a baseball game are those who know the game well. The people who like cooking shows on television are people who cook.

We can be at a baseball game and know the rules, but unless we're a student of that sport, we're unlikely to appreciate a particular situation.

We can watch a cooking show on television and know our way around the kitchen a bit, but unless we've tried to make a soufflé and failed or been looking for new recipes or time-saving techniques, we're unlikely to stick with that channel.

That doesn't mean we have to be experts at either one.

And, in the same way, we don't have to be theologians or Scripture scholars, we don't have to be saints to learn more about the Mass and so begin to better appreciate the Mass.

Better take advantage of its truly limitless advantages.

Where to begin? You already have. We begin by wanting more. We're never being greedy when we ask God for more faith, more hope, more love. We're never being selfish when we ask him to help us become better at praying, better at loving.

We begin getting more out of Mass by taking more to Mass. Part of what we can bring is newfound knowledge because with that, most times, comes newfound appreciation. We appreciate more. Not just the many traditions that have been a part of the development of the Mass. Not just the rich history that has brought it to where it is today. We appreciate how we fit into those traditions and history. We appreciate what we are saying and doing there. And why we are saying and doing those things.

And we appreciate more the role of the Holy Spirit not just at Mass but in the history, tradition and development of the Mass itself. The Spirit's role in the history, tradition and development of the Church.

The role that same Spirit is offering to play in our own lives. In your life.

Jesus left us a treasure: His presence in a special way in the Eucharist. Too often our day-to-day busy-ness, our short-sightedness, our ignoring the call of the Creator, keep us from realizing its worth.

But then, too, to be fair, we can make the mistake of thinking the Mass is common because, for most of us, it's so readily available. It's so relatively easy to get to a Mass, if we choose to. Again, that's for most of us. Those who have lived or now live under conditions where the Mass is outlawed or restricted would have a different perspective.

Hold on, though. If Jesus is present in the Eucharist, and he is, then shouldn't we Catholics spend *all* our time in church? All our time at Mass or on our knees before the Blessed Sacrament, the consecrated host reserved in the tabernacle?

No, because at the end of each Mass we're sent out. Not "back into" the world. The Mass is part of this world. We're sent out to discover, and rediscover, how we are to love others and to live that Christian life.

Fortunately, we have the examples of people who have done that. We have the stories and the writings of people just like us who realized what the Mass is, and lived their lives accordingly. They are our saints, those men, women and children recognized by the Church for their ability to love and serve God and others.

Each of them, at some point, made the Mass his own or her own. Just as each of us is called to do the same. At some point, we have to start to grow up spiritually. We choose to go to Mass because *we* choose to go to Mass. We're there because we want to be there, because we realize in so many ways we need to be there.

We're there even when, as some saints put it, we're experiencing the "dark night of the soul." Our prayers seem empty. Our hope is dim, if not completely gone. Even then, we begin to understand that we don't attend Mass simply so we'll *feel* better. Sometimes we don't feel better.

We attend Mass to *make* us better. To heal us, yes, but more than in the sense of good health. To make us better by helping shape us in the image which God intended. In the Book of Genesis, the story of creation says God formed Adam from dust (see Gn 2:7). He formed us, too. God shaped us, and shapes us, but we also play a role in shaping ourselves. (Free will, remember?)

"Be patient, God isn't through with me yet" was a popular expression in some circles. That's true enough. But what we may not realize is part of that completion is up to us. He's not responsible for the whole project. Why not? Again, because he loves us so much.

The Mass is further proof, to take that analogy just one step further, that he's an on-site foreman. We each may have tasks to do but he's always right there, ready to be called on. No, he won't take over and do them for us. But he will be right there, offering his help and his encouragement.

At the Mass, we can come into direct, personal contact with the Way, with the Truth and with the Life (see Jn 14:6).

That's what happens at every Mass. We have the potential to be a part of all that right now. And become more a part of it each time we're there. It's ours for the asking, ours for the taking. Freely given. Offered to you with infinite love.

In This Book

The Mass is relatively simple. In later chapters, we'll examine the various parts, how they developed and how they all fit together. And the Mass is complex, beyond our ability to understand. It's more than the sum of those parts. It's the Real Presence of the Creator of the universe in a unique and particular way of the universe.

As the *Catechism* explains, since the time of the apostles, the Mass, the Eucharist (from the Greek for "thanksgiving") has been and "remains the center of the Church's life" (*CCC* 1343).

But what is it? That's what we'll look at in this book. First, though, we should do a little defining. What's the difference between the *Mass* and the *Eucharist*? It can be confusing because the Mass is referred to as the Eucharist. And Holy Communion, receiving Jesus under the appearances of bread and wine, is also called that. So, it's possible to "receive the Eucharist at the Eucharist."

It's possible to go to Mass and not receive Holy Communion. And it's possible to receive Holy Communion outside of Mass. A youngster may go to Mass for a number of years before being old enough to receive Communion.

When we refer to the Eucharist and mean Communion, we're talking about a sacrament. There are seven sacraments: baptism, reconciliation (penance or confession), the Eucharist, confirmation, marriage, ordination and anointing of the sick.

The sacraments, the *Catechism* says, "are efficacious [that is, effective] signs of grace, instituted by Christ and entrusted to the Church, by which divine life is dispensed to us. The visible rites by which the sacraments are celebrated signify and make present the graces proper to each sacrament. They bear fruit in those who receive them with the required dispositions" (*CCC* 1131).

Let's break that down. Christ began the sacraments and gave them to the Church. There are specific words and actions for each. Each gives grace and can transform, can better, the person who properly receives it.

So when the *Catechism* talks about the Eucharist, it begins by noting that it, along with baptism and confirmation, "completes Christian initiation" (*CCC* 1322). "Those who have been raised to the dignity of the royal priesthood by Baptism [this doesn't mean being ordained; all baptized people share in

Christ's priesthood] and configured more deeply to Christ by Confirmation participate with the whole community in the Lord's own sacrifice by means of the Eucharist" (*CCC* 1322).

The *Catechism* goes on to say that at the Last Supper Jesus instituted the Eucharistic sacrifice of his Body and Blood. He did this to perpetuate the sacrifice of the cross throughout the ages until he should come again, and to entrust to "his beloved Spouse, the Church, a memorial of his death and resurrection: a sacrament of love, a sign of unity, a bond of charity, a Paschal [Passover/Easter] banquet 'in which Christ is consumed, the mind is filled with grace and a pledge of future glory is given to us.'"[4]

Let's say that again. A memorial of his death and resurrection. A sacrament of love. A sign of unity. A bond of charity. A Paschal banquet.

And at this celebration: The mind is filled with grace. And a pledge of future glory is given to us. That is, heaven.

All that? Every Sunday at 8:30, 10 and 11:45?

Yes. At each Mass. At every Mass. Because the Eucharist is "the source and summit of Christian life."[5] It's at the very heart of Catholicism because "the other sacraments, and indeed all ecclesiastical ministries and works of the apostolate [everything the Church does], are bound up with the Eucharist and are oriented toward it."

Why? Why all that at one event?

Because "in the blessed Eucharist is contained the whole spiritual good of the Church, namely Christ himself."[6] But, as we'll see in the next chapter, the Mass traces its history back to more than a millennium before the birth of Christ.

Q. & A.:
What is "Transubstantiation"?

What is transubstantiation?
That's the term used to describe what happens to the host and the wine at Mass. They change in substance, not in form. What they *are* changes. How they look, feel and taste don't.

Is this what Jesus called it?
No, although the Real Presence of Christ in the Eucharist was a fundamental doctrine from apostolic times. It was, after all, what he told his apostles at the Last Supper. But the term wasn't adopted by the Church until the Fourth Lateran Council in 1215.

So is Jesus not at a Mass until the consecration?
God is everywhere. The Second Person of the Blessed Trinity is in the Eucharist in a unique way. Pope Paul VI (1963–1978—dates for popes in this book are the years of their pontificate) put it this way: "The presence of Christ in the Eucharist is called the Real Presence not to exclude the other kinds as though they were not real, but because it is real *par excellence*, since it is substantial, in the sense the Christ whole and entire, God and man, becomes present" (from his encyclical "On the Holy Eucharist"). In addition to the presence in the Eucharist, Vatican II stated that Christ is present in the assembly, in the Word and in the person of the priest.

So does the Mass "create" Jesus?

The Body and Blood of Christ already exist. Jesus is in his glorified state, his risen body, and he doesn't "leave" heaven to be in the Eucharist. Transubstantiation means the bread and wine are changed into his Body and Blood. Nothing of the substance of bread and wine remain. They have been completely replaced by Jesus' already existing Body and Blood.

Is that understandable?

We can describe what happens and who causes it to happen but we can't explain how it happens, in physical terms. If we look at it logically, it makes little sense. We Catholics can't prove it, like a lawyer would prove his case or a scientist prove her theory.

It's been a "hard" teaching since the time of Christ. "How can this man give us his flesh to eat?" some Jews asked when Jesus spoke of himself as "the bread of life." That encounter can be found in John 6:35-58.

The evangelist notes that "because of this many of his disciples turned back and no longer went about with him" (v. 66). (They also didn't like what he had to say about the cross and dying.) He asked the apostles point-blank if they were going to do the same. Peter responded: "Lord, to whom can we go? You have the words of eternal life" (v. 68).

And the Church still teaches that?

Yes. As the *Catechism* explains: "The Council of Trent [1545–1563] summarizes the Catholic faith by declaring:

'Because Christ our Redeemer said that it was truly his body that he was offering under the species of bread, it has always been the conviction of the Church of God, and this holy Council now declares again, that by the consecration of the bread and wine there takes place a change of the whole substance of the bread into the Body of Christ our Lord and of the whole substance of the wine into the substance of his Blood. This change the holy Catholic Church has fittingly and properly called "transubstantiation."'[7]

The *Catechism* goes on to say that the Eucharistic presence of Christ starts at the moment of consecration and remains as long as the Eucharistic species subsist. It adds that Christ is present whole and entire in each of the species, and whole and entire in each of their parts, in such a way that the breaking of the bread doesn't "divide" Christ.

And Jesus is present in both species, his Body and his Blood. His Blood is also present in the consecrated bread, his Body also in the consecrated wine.

CHAPTER TWO

Our Jewish Roots

It's impossible to closely examine the Mass today without looking carefully at an event that happened more than three thousand years ago.

That's because our celebration traces its roots back to the Last Supper, Jesus' final meal with his apostles before his crucifixion. And *that* dinner, at which he *instituted* the Eucharist (in other words, at the world's first "Mass") traces *its* roots back to the feast of Passover, almost thirteen hundred years before Christ.

What was the feast of Passover all about? And, for Jews today, what is it still all about?

Maybe it's best to begin at ... the beginning. Some thirty-eight hundred years ago God intervened in human history in a special way when he visited a man named Abram. That story can be found in Genesis 12-25.

God made a deal with Abram. A covenant. A contract. Abram would do this and God would do that. And after they made the deal, God changed Abram's name to "Abraham," meaning "ancestor of a multitude."

Why did God step in? Simply put, we humans had messed up. Since the time of our first parents, we had been sinning. We had not severed our relationship with our Creator but we had severely damaged it. God still loved us. We had trouble loving him. But God never abandoned us. He always wanted only the best for us. He still does.

At a time when people believed in many deities, God told Abraham to worship him alone. And as a sign of their belief in the Lord, Abraham and his descendants were to follow particular rules and commit particular acts. (Every male had to be circumcised, for example.) And God would see to it that Abraham had land and countless descendants.

God made Abraham the *father* of the Hebrews. And it was the Hebrews—the Jews, including Jesus—who came to celebrate Passover.

You may be familiar with some names from the Old Testament. Abraham was the father of Isaac. Isaac was the father of Jacob. Later, God would visit Jacob and change his name to Israel. Israel would have twelve sons, the "twelve tribes of Israel."

Not surprisingly, the brothers didn't always get along. And ten of them especially didn't like Joseph, Jacob's favorite.

What does all this have to do with the Mass? A lot. Hang in there.

Genesis 37 tells how the brothers decided to kill Joseph but then changed their minds and sold him into slavery. He ended up in Egypt where he prospered. In fact, he became one of Pharaoh's top aides. He advised the leader to prepare for a famine and so, when hard times hit, the country was ready. Other places and people weren't as fortunate. That was why his brothers came to Egypt. They were looking for grain.

The siblings didn't recognize Joseph but he could tell who they were. Eventually, the whole family—including the father—ended up there. All was forgiven and everything was great. For a while.

Genesis concludes with the death of Joseph, and the next book, Exodus, quickly points out that "now a new king arose over Egypt, who did not know Joseph." Worse still, from the Egyptian point of view, there were more Israelites than Egyptians and, in reality, they had more power. So the Egyptian officials made the visitors slaves. They "set taskmasters over them to oppress them with forced labor" (Ex 1:11).

It's a familiar story, one that's been replayed countless ways in countless countries down through the centuries. And then, as now, some of it's grisly.

The king instructed Hebrew midwives to kill all Hebrew males at birth. But they ignored his command because they feared God more than any king. So the pharaoh ordered every infant Hebrew boy thrown into the Nile.

It was at this point that Moses was born. His mother kept him hidden for three months and then set him in a watertight basket in the reeds along the river. When Pharaoh's daughter came down to the river to bathe, she discovered the basket. Moses' sister, who had been watching all this unfold, stepped forward and offered to find a nurse to take care of the child for Pharaoh's daughter. The sister got her—and Moses'—mother. The princess paid Moses' mother to take care of the boy until he was older and then "she took him as her son" (Ex 2:10).

Those first chapters of Exodus also explain how Moses ended up killing an Egyptian and fleeing for his life. They tell how God spoke to him in a bush that was "blazing" but wasn't being consumed by the fire.

Bottom line: God wanted Moses to go back to Egypt and lead his—the Lord's—people out of slavery.

Not surprisingly, Moses wasn't thrilled with the idea, even after God performed miracles for him. No offense, God, he argued, but "I have never been eloquent, neither in the past nor even now that you have spoken to your servant; but I am slow of speech and slow of tongue" (Ex 4:10). Couldn't the Lord send someone else? No, God replied, but I will let you take along your brother Aaron.

So Moses tells the Egyptian leader: "Thus says the Lord, the God of Israel, 'Let my people go...'" (Ex 5:1).

It comes as no shock that Pharaoh considered Moses' request an insult. No way, Moses. In fact, the ruler made the Hebrew slaves work harder.

Moses' miracles didn't change the pharaoh's mind. And neither did a series of "plagues": water turned to blood; infestations of frogs, gnats and flies; livestock stricken with disease; boils on humans and animals; swarms of locusts; and darkness for three days.

All that set the stage for the first Passover.

The Ultimate Plague, the First Passover

The final plague, the clincher, was horrible. God sent Moses to warn Pharaoh that every firstborn in Egypt was going to die at about midnight. Every single one. From the household of the king to that of the lowliest slave. And the same with all the first-born of the livestock. But the Israelites would be spared. The people and their animals.

And then, Moses said, the country's leaders will beg me to lead the Israelites out of Egypt. The author of Exodus notes, "in hot anger he [Moses] left Pharaoh" (Ex 11:8).

God told Moses and Aaron how the Israelites were to prepare for that awful night. That month was to become the first month of the year for them. On the tenth day, they were to take a lamb for each family, each household. It was to be without blemish, a one-year-old male, a sheep or a goat.

On the fourteenth day, at twilight, all were to slaughter their lambs and take some of the blood and put it on the two door posts and lintel—the top part of the door—of the house in which they were going to eat.

They were to eat the lamb that night. Roasted. With unleavened bread and bitter herbs. It was to be cooked whole, with its head, legs and inner organs. If anything was left over, it was to be burned up before morning.

And this was how they were to eat it: Loins girded, ready for travel. With sandals on their feet and staffs in their hands. They were to eat quickly.

"It is the passover of the Lord," says Exodus 12:11-13. "For I will pass through the land of Egypt that night, and I will strike down every firstborn in the land of Egypt, both human beings and animals; on all the gods of Egypt I will execute judgments: I am the Lord. The blood shall be a sign for you on the houses where you live: when I see the blood, I will pass over you, and no plague shall destroy you when I strike the land of Egypt."

More than that, "This day shall be a day of remembrance for you," God continued. "You shall celebrate it as a festival to the Lord; throughout your generations you shall observe it as a perpetual ordinance" (v. 14).

Also, for "seven days you shall eat unleavened bread" (v. 15). That meant, for the week following Passover, they were to eat nothing with yeast in it.

The tenth and final plague happened the way Moses had described. Among the Egyptians, no household was spared. Then Pharaoh summoned Moses and Aaron during the night and told them to take the Israelites and leave.

We know now that the Israelites' pilgrimage was no walk in

the park. Although the distance—if traveled directly—is only some 250 miles, the Exodus took forty years. An entire generation was born and reached adulthood before that journey ended.

And during those years, at times the people turned against Moses and "his" God. And during those years, God revealed more of himself to his people.

His "chosen people." The people he was preparing for the coming of his Son.

That preparation would continue for another twelve and a half centuries.

Enter Jesus

This was the culture, the religion, into which Jesus was born and raised. He was a Jew who could trace his ancestry back to David, the great king. He was a devout follower who observed the commandments of God and the practices of Judaism.

We have to keep in mind that Jesus knew when he was going to die. Knew how he was going to die. He told his followers what was going to happen to him. And while he didn't welcome it, he accepted it. "Abba, Father," he prayed in the garden before he was arrested, "for you all things are possible; remove this cup from me; yet, not what I want, but what you want" (Mk 14:36).

That's another reason the Last Supper is such a powerful—and moving—event.

There's a question, a kind of game, we sometimes like to ask each other today. "If you knew you had only one day to live, how would you spend it?" Obviously, the answer is supposed to reveal something about ourselves. What we value most. What we've neglected or want to set right.

The Gospels tell us how Jesus answered that question.

"On the first day of Unleavened Bread, when the Passover lamb is sacrificed," Mark says, the disciples asked Jesus where he wanted them to go and get ready for the special meal. (That begins with Mark 14:12. It can also be found starting in Matthew 26:17 and Luke 22:7.)

Jesus sent two of them off into Jerusalem with instructions to follow a man carrying a jar of water. They were to go to the house he entered and say to the owner that "The Teacher asks, Where is my guest room where I may eat the Passover with my disciples?" (v. 14).

The "Upper Room" would become central to the early Church. (*Go to: Q. & A.: "Where Was the Upper Room?"*)

What the evangelists say about that meal—about the core of what happened on that evening—is the same. But the retelling isn't identical. That shouldn't surprise us. Each writer had a unique voice. Each had a particular audience. Each wrote at a distinct moment in those early years of the Church.

They do agree that this was a Passover meal (whether or not it was Passover itself). The formula, the ritual, that went back to Moses and the chosen people enslaved in Egypt was reenacted on that evening. God's saving the Jewish people was remembered.

Luke says it was Peter and John, two prominent apostles, who were sent to find the fellow carrying the jar of water. This would be a big container drawn from a community well, not some tiny receptacle holding only a liter or two. Luke is also the one who tells us that on that evening Jesus let his apostles know what was on his mind.

"I have eagerly desired to eat this Passover with you before I suffer" (Lk 22:15). He wasn't going to eat again, he added, until "it is fulfilled in the kingdom of God." Until he had done what he had come to earth to do.

While Jesus' words may have seemed confusing—and frightening—to his followers, his actions up until then weren't. Certainly each of these men had sat through many a Passover meal.

They knew about the whole lamb, the bitter herbs, the unleavened bread. They knew about eating while being ready to go. They knew about the various cups of wine. They knew the prayers. They knew the story that wasn't just being told but was being reenacted. (*Go to: Q. & A.: "The Seder, Then and Now."*)

And then Jesus changed the script. At the end of the meal, he took a loaf of bread "and when he had given thanks, he broke it and gave it to them, saying 'This is my body, which is given for you. Do this in remembrance of me'" (Lk 22:19).

Then he "did the same with the cup after supper, saying, 'This cup that is poured out for you is the new covenant in my blood'" (Lk 22:20).

This is my body. This unleavened bread.

This is my blood. This cup of wine.

Do this—do what?—in memory of him.

What could it mean? What was he saying?

In other passages, the evangelists note that sometimes the apostles just didn't get Jesus' message. Sometimes they asked him to explain it for them. Sometimes they didn't. But there was no time for asking that night. After the meal, Jesus headed off to pray. That wasn't unusual. They knew he spent nights in prayer.

What they didn't know—what they surely couldn't have

guessed—was that his prayers in the Garden of Gethsemane would be followed by his arrest, his torture, his trial and his execution.

In less than twenty-four hours, as far as the apostles could tell, Jesus was gone. And they had every reason to believe the authorities might hunt them down and do the same to them.

But Jesus had *told* them he was leaving, hadn't he? Told them he was going to die. They just couldn't, just wouldn't, believe it.

That bread was his body. That wine was his blood.

They were supposed to do the same in memory of him.

Just as the Israelites remembered being delivered from slavery, being spared from death, with the Passover feast, now the apostles were supposed to remember ... what?

We like to think that if we had seen Jesus during his public life—during the three years he preached and healed—we would have immediately recognized him as the Messiah and would have eagerly joined his followers. But what we tend to forget, what we can easily overlook, is that we know how the story ends.

We know that after the Last Supper, after Good Friday, after that Sabbath when his cold, stiff body lay in the tomb, he came back to life. We know there was an Easter.

The apostles didn't. The other disciples, those who weren't part of the Twelve, didn't. All the twelve knew was one of their own, Judas, had arranged for Jesus to be arrested. One of their own, Peter, who was supposed to be their leader, denied even knowing him. Denied him not once, not twice, but three times.

Betrayed and denied, just as Jesus had predicted.

Did the apostles feel "delivered"? Did they feel "saved"? It doesn't seem likely since ten apparently were in hiding and one had committed suicide (Judas, who hanged himself). Only John found the courage to stand at the foot of the cross.

What had happened at the Last Supper? What had Jesus meant?

We have the advantage here. After the promised Holy Spirit came, after Pentecost, the apostles began to comprehend Christ's words. They began to realize and accept what it was they were to do. And they began to do it.

The Holy Spirit is with the Church, with us, still. And we have some two thousand years of teaching to help us realize how much was going on at that final meal.

As the *Catechism of the Catholic Church* puts it: "By celebrating the Last Supper with his apostles in the course of the Passover meal, Jesus gave the Jewish Passover its definitive meaning. Jesus' passing over to the father by his death and Resurrection, the new Passover, is anticipated in the Supper and celebrated in the Eucharist, which fulfills the Jewish Passover and anticipates the final Passover of the Church in the glory of the kingdom" (1340).

The old Passover used a lamb—a "paschal" lamb, with that word coming from the Greek for Passover—and unleavened bread. The new Passover centers on the Lamb of God (a title we use three times in a row shortly before Holy Communion) whose Body and Blood are present in the consecrated bread and wine.

At the Last Supper, for the first time, Jesus gives himself as the Bread of Life.

"I am the bread of life," he had told the people (Jn 6:35). "Whoever comes to me will never be hungry, and whoever believes in me will never be thirsty."

Nonsense, some of the people had answered.

But that was what he did at the Last Supper. It's what he has done at every Mass since then. It's what he continues to do.

Q. & A.:
Where Was the Upper Room?

Whose house had the Upper Room?

Traditionally, historians have said that the Upper Room most likely belonged to one of Jesus' disciples, but the Gospels don't give a name.

They've speculated the room was large and furnished for dining.

Did anything else happen there?

It was the same spot where Jesus showed himself to the apostles after his Resurrection, the place where the apostle Matthias was chosen to replace Judas, and the room in which the apostles hid until the Holy Spirit blew through it on Pentecost.

For a time, the historians maintain, it was the only church—in the sense of a meeting place—in Jerusalem. Later, early Christians would meet in homes not in buildings erected or set aside just for worship.

What became of the room itself?

Historians also say St. Paula of Rome visited this "Church of the Apostles" or "Church of Zion" in 404. And it was destroyed by the Saracens, the Moslems at the time of the Crusades, in the 11th century. Later it was rebuilt and put under the care of the Augustinians, a religious order. Destroyed and rebuilt again, it was placed under the jurisdiction of the Franciscans who were forced out in 1561. Now it is a mosque.

What about the "Upper Room" in Jerusalem today?

Today tourists visit *an* upper room while in Jerusalem but, obviously, it's not a first-century Palestinian building.

The Seder, Then and Now

The Jewish festival of Pesach ("passing over" or "protecting") begins with the fifteenth and ends with the twenty-first day of the month of Nisan. That's in March or April.

On those seven days all leaven in bread or any other food is forbidden but unleavened bread—"matzo"—may be eaten. Sometimes Passover is called the Festival of Unleavened Bread.

The special family meal on the fifteenth is called the *seder*—Hebrew for "order." Jews living outside of Israel celebrate for eight days and have a seder for the first two nights.

Seder begins with the head of the family blessing the holiday with a prayer over a cup of wine. The entire meal includes four cups of wine which are drunk at certain points during the evening.

After all the participants have washed their hands, the leader offers them celery or another raw vegetable dipped in vinegar or salt water. Next a shank bone (symbolic of the Paschal lamb) and, frequently in recent times, a hard-boiled egg (a symbol of God's kindness or, some say, a sad reminder of the destruction of the Temple of Jerusalem) are taken from the seder plate.

While that takes place, the participants are reciting a prayer.

After the second cup of wine is poured, the youngest child asks four standard questions about why this night differs from all other nights.

- Why only unleavened bread?
- Why only bitter herbs?
- Why dip those herbs twice?
- Why do all eat reclining?

The set responses—recited in unison—offer the spiritual interpretations of the customs even though, historians say, some aspects of those customs copied Greco-Roman banquets.

The key is the Haggadah, the story of the Exodus.

At this point, once again, all the participants wash their hands. Then they eat the matzo and bitter herbs dipped into a mixture of crushed fruit and wine, showing that freedom and spiritual growth are the reward of suffering and sacrifice.

Then the meal is eaten.

Following prayers, a third cup—a cup of thanksgiving to God—is poured. Psalms of praise are recited and a fourth cup of wine—to God's loving providence—is poured. Some add a fifth, not consumed, in honor of the prophet Elijah, whose appearance at some future seder will mark the coming of the Messiah.

Sometimes folk songs are sung after the meal.

CHAPTER THREE

Getting in Shape Over Centuries

A first-century Christian might have a hard time recognizing today's parish Sunday liturgy as the same celebration he or she knows. Then again, even though much has changed, the essence of the Mass has—amazingly, miraculously—remained the same since those early years.

The flip side is also true. Suddenly transported back to the time of the apostles, we might not realize a Mass is being celebrated until the consecration is reached.

Even that term—"Mass"—was unheard of back then. (*Go to: "Q. & A.: How Did the Mass Get Its Name?"*)

"The breaking of the bread," as it's called in Acts 2:42-46, took place in private homes. And the basic outline for the service, in the style of the Passover meal, included:

• A benediction calling people to praise God.
• A reminder of God's goodness.
• Another benediction that included a "doxology"—a formula of praise, such as "Glory to the Father and to the Son and to the Holy Spirit."

Just as in the Passover meal, at this early Mass bread and wine were blessed. In the Jewish rite at that time, the leader prayed: "Blessed are you, Lord our God, eternal king, for bringing forth bread from the earth." And "Blessed are you, Lord our God, eternal king, for making the fruit of the vine."

In our own time, the priest at Mass prays: "Blessed are you, Lord God of all creation, through your goodness we have this bread to offer, which earth has given and human hands have made." And "Blessed are you, Lord God of all creation, through your goodness we have this wine to offer, fruit of the vine and work of human hands."

At Mass, the priest adds to the first prayer: "It will become for us the bread of life." And to the second: "It will become our spiritual drink."

At the Passover meal, the bread and wine remain bread and wine. Not so at the Lord's Supper. That was the common name for the ceremony held by those who had been baptized. But *ceremony* may be too stuffy a word. It really was a communal celebration. Or, rather, celebrations.

Originally there were two services. The Liturgy of the Word—which included readings from Scripture and a homily—was held on Saturday morning, the "Sabbath." (*Go to: "When Did Sunday Become the Sabbath?"*) But the Eucharist was something else. This had two parts: a shared meal and the Eucharist itself. That shared meal, called *agape* (pronounced AH-ga-pay) from the Greek word for *love,* presented some problems. Some abuses cropped up and so it was soon separated from the Eucharist.

One element of the meal remained. Where in the past, the celebration was in a dining hall, now only one table was used and the character of the assembly changed from diners to worshipers.

The New Testament describes those earliest years. Outside Scripture, a document called the *Didache,* which was probably written in Syria around A.D. 60, is another record of those times. "Now about the Eucharist," it says, "this is how to give thanks." It goes on to share some prayers and some blessings from a strong Jewish heritage.

By the middle of the second century the Mass had taken on a more definite structure. The agape—that potluck before the Eucharist—was out and the Liturgy of the Word was in.

And, early on, these Eucharistic gatherings were held in the early morning and, eventually, on Sunday because that was the day on which Jesus rose from the dead (see Jn 20:1).

The Mass remained a communal celebration presided over by the community's leader, the bishop. But as the Church grew and more groups formed, the bishop's delegate—a priest—began to take his place at some Masses. (In chapter 5 we'll look at how a remnant of that transition remains in the Mass today.)

In the beginning, there was no set Eucharistic prayer or canon. Yes, they followed Jewish canons but a bishop was free to pray the way he wanted to. Naturally, over time some patterns developed. And those bishops who were less gifted at coming up with spontaneous prayer began to use texts written by others.

In "The First Apology," St. Justin Martyr describes the structure that had developed. (Here "apology" doesn't mean saying you're sorry. It means defending one's beliefs.) Around the year 150, an outline for the Mass went this way:

- Scripture readings
- homily
- prayers
- Kiss of Peace
- offertory
- Eucharistic prayer which the congregation concluded with an "amen"
- Holy Communion

Add in "passing out bulletins after the service" and then "serving folks coffee and doughnuts in the hall" and we could be talking about just about any parish today. (*Go to: "Justin Martyr on the Mass."*)

But, again, it isn't just the form that's ancient. It's the formula—the words themselves. Historians point out that while St. Justin Martyr tended to speak in generalities, St. Hippolytus (c.170-236) was much more specific. They note that this Roman priest and martyr wrote down a Eucharistic prayer from his time that was used in our day as the model for the Roman Catholic Church's Eucharistic Prayer II. Well, some say he wrote it. Others say it was based on his writing but wasn't penned until the middle of the fourth century.

They do agree there was a monumental shift in the life of the Church in the early part of that century. For its first three hundred years, Christianity had been against Roman law. It was an offense punishable by death. It was why there were so many martyrs in those early years including, tradition says, all of the apostles except John.

But in 313, with the Edict of Milan, Emperor Constantine changed that law. In fact, the pendulum went swinging in the other direction. Christianity became the "in" religion. Until then it made sense that Mass was celebrated in homes and halls and catacombs (those burial caves used by Christians and non-Christians alike in a number of places around the Mediterranean). After the Edict of Milan, the Church no longer needed to remain underground—figuratively or literally. And the emperors, showing their support for it, began to give it gifts of land and buildings. Now the people could gather in great churches in greater numbers.

Which was wonderful, of course. Magnificent structures

could be built and Christians could worship openly and without fear. But it wasn't so wonderful, too. Bigger buildings and bigger crowds chipped away at that sense of community, that sense of fellowship, that had been a hallmark of earlier Masses.

We've all experienced that in our own time. Mass at a small country parish can have a different "feel" than Mass at a large urban or suburban one. A good comparison might be shopping at a mom-and-pop store and going to a mall. In either parish setting, of course, the Mass is the Mass.

Traditions and Changes

Historians say a couple of traditions continued. One was a Sunday rather than daily celebration. Daily would become common later. The other was taking home the consecrated bread after Mass (there were no tabernacles) and keeping it there, with all due respect and reverence. This was for reception of Communion at home and for taking the Eucharist to the homebound, to prisoners and to hermits. But as the Mass became what we might call more impersonal, as worshipers became more audience than active participants, attendance fell and reception of the Eucharist dropped.

In all fairness, it needs to be added that once Christianity was legalized and getting baptized was considered a smart move politically, some folks joined the Church with less zeal than had those before 313. Before it meant being an outlaw, and was seen as a serious, and dangerous, step. After it became politically correct, to put it crassly, for some people it was more like joining the right country club to get ahead socially or at work.

There was another major change in the fourth century. Until

384, the prayers of the Mass were in Greek because that was the official language of the Church. Which only made sense because most people spoke Greek. Or, rather, most *had* spoken Greek until then, when Latin gained dominance. So Pope Damasus changed the language of the Mass to Latin. It would remain the standard for almost sixteen centuries. It wasn't until the Second Vatican Council (1962-1965) that the Mass and other liturgical celebrations would be said in the vernacular—that is, the common language of the local people.

Another element that was pretty much set by the fourth century was the Roman Canon, the Eucharistic prayer. In fact, it was the only one for the next fifteen hundred-plus years until Vatican II, when a number of other canons were allowed.

Historians say the reign of Pope St. Gregory the Great (590-604) is the next milestone in the development of the Mass. He's credited with making the first reforms, changes he thought necessary for that time.

Gregory made the Mass more solemn. More prayers and chants and particular gestures were grafted on to the traditional form. And since Rome was the center of the Church in the West, that set the tone for all other western bishops and priests. The goal wasn't to make the Mass lofty, historians say, but to help people better understand what was truly happening at every Eucharistic celebration.

It wasn't Gregory's reforms that brought about an even bigger change in the Mass, they add, but the spread of heresy.

There were a number of well-known heresies in those early centuries, and Church councils—gatherings of the bishops—were called to deal with them. One major heresy was Arianism. Arius was a fourth-century priest of Alexandria, Egypt, who taught that Jesus was human only, not God. This view gained wide popularity and so the bishops met in Nicaea (what is now Turkey) in 325 to set the teaching straight: Jesus was—is—both human and divine.

But because they were combating the notion of humanity-only, they tended to stress the divine. The Nicene Creed was added to the Mass. So were more prayers to the Trinity, the Three Divine Persons, the Father, Son and Holy Spirit. There was a new emphasis on the fact that no one was worthy of receiving Christ in the Eucharist. (We still say that before Communion. It's still true.)

"Listen up, people," the Church said. "Do you realize what is *really* going on at Mass?"

Small wonder there was a new remoteness and a new emphasis on cleanliness. Absolutions and ablutions (washings) were added. And the custom of receiving Holy Communion in the hands was eliminated. How could some local worker with dirt engrained in his fingers and palms dare to hold God!

Even the bread itself was changed. What originally had been a matzo was replaced by a host.

Prior to the Gregorian Sacramentary—the liturgical book put together by Pope St. Gregory the Great—there were what we might call different versions of the Mass. And even immediately after that, no pope declared *this* was the one and only way the liturgy could be celebrated. A number of books were used, even in Rome itself.

Then came Charlemagne. Crowned first emperor of the Holy Roman Empire in 800, he thought one way to bring greater uniformity to his kingdom was to bring greater uniformity to the way the Mass was celebrated. So liturgical books became more alike and ceremonies became more lofty. By the eleventh century, the papal way dominated. There were only pockets where a different liturgy was used in Italy and Spain. In the thirteenth century, the followers of the new religious order founded by St. Francis of Assisi promoted and spread the Roman sacramentary by using it as they traveled and preached throughout the West.

(All this refers to the West. In the East, in Constantinople— now Istanbul, Turkey—the liturgy was developing in another way. Yes, it was the Mass, rooted in the Last Supper, but how the bishops and priests celebrated there was different from how their counterparts did in the West. That's still the case.)

More Priests Meant More Masses

The monks also influenced the development of the Mass. St. Benedict is regarded as the founder of monasticism in the West. In the sixth century, he wrote a *Rule* for his monks at Monte Cassino, Italy, which came to be used at monasteries throughout Europe. Prior to that there had been various groups that traced their roots to early-century hermits living in the desert. Originally, most monasteries had only a few priests. Most members were brothers. They had taken vows of poverty, chastity and obedience, but they weren't ordained. They weren't priests. And only a priest can celebrate Mass.

As more priests were ordained to be sent out for missionary work, and there were more priests within a single community, private Masses began to be said. A private Mass was one at which there was no congregation. Unlike today, when a con-celebrated Mass can have a main celebrant and any number of concelebrants, back then it was one priest/one Mass.

So the other priests would say private Masses, not infrequently in private chapels or at side altars. This practice continued even through the twentieth century until Vatican II. Up until the last half of the twentieth century, a monastery or seminary would have a main chapel for the community Mass and then a honeycomb of tiny chapels where a priest could say Mass privately with only one or two altar boys.

A second development in the Middle Ages (the Middle Ages extended from about 500 to 1500) was the idea of a votive Mass. This meant the Mass was said for a special intention. For a deceased loved one, for someone who was sick, for someone celebrating a birthday and so on. While that makes perfect sense—we pray for each other all the time—it was an idea that became overemphasized and tended to blur the basic meaning of the Mass.

During that period, the dominant belief was the Mass was where you asked for something special. Or you got together with like-minded folks—in a guild or confraternity—and had Masses for

When Did Sunday Become the Sabbath?

The Book of Genesis says God created the universe in six days. Beginning on the first day of the week, Sunday, and ending on the last, the Saturday, on which he rested.

"Sabbath" comes for the Hebrew word for resting or ceasing. In Jesus' time—and even today—there are serious restrictions among Jews concerning what can and cannot be done on the Sabbath.

But, over time, Christians began celebrating on the first day of the week because Jesus rose from the dead on Sunday and it was on Sunday that the Holy Spirit descended on the apostles on Pentecost.

your group. This upped the demand for the number of Masses, especially as requests increased for the repose of the souls of dead loved ones.

Again, this wasn't a bad, or wrong, idea. The Mass is certainly the best way to pray. And who wouldn't want the best for his or her intention? But "the best way to pray" sometimes slipped into "the fastest way to get grace." That is, to receive God's special blessing and favor. No longer a community celebration, the liturgy was becoming more mechanical: Do this, this and this and you received God's grace for your intention.

No congregation was necessary. Not even the person or group who had requested the Mass. The priest could do it all alone or with a single altar server. Naturally, Father would handle all the readings since it was unlikely a server could read. And he sang alone if there was any singing. With no congregation, there was no reason to have a big chapel. Those side altars or tiny, private chapels worked just fine. And since they were so small, he wasn't able to move around much. Instead he moved the book from one side of the altar to the other. There wasn't any need for a lot of different liturgical books. All the parts of the Mass could be put in a single, handy volume called a missal. After the thirteenth century it was *the* book for saying Mass.

Saying, not celebrating. *Celebrating* hardly described the action of the priest, quickly and quietly going through the actions and prayers, being careful not to disturb his fellow priests doing the same at nearby side altars.

That sense of privacy and even secrecy soon crept into community Masses, too. In the past, the people's *amen*—meaning Yes! or So be it!—at the end of the canon was said with gusto. Now the eucharistic prayer was whispered by the priest. By the year 1000, it was the way priests were supposed to pray it.

And the people ...

The people watched, even at the Sunday Mass said at a cathedral's main altar. The table, the remnant from the shared meal of earlier times, stopped being a free-standing piece of furniture and was attached to a wall. It had been against a decorated wall since the sixth century in the West and, apparently, from the beginning in the East. By 1000, that was standard. Candles were added a century later. Historians say it was a reminder of Mass in the catacombs. And a cross was included on the altar around 1300.

Putting both priest and people on the same side—facing East, the direction in which, it was believed, Christ would return—was seen as symbolic of both acting as one. But what separated the celebrant from the congregation was an altar rail. It divided the sanctuary from the nave, the main part of the church. And divided the priest from the people.

Over time, the people began to receive Holy Communion under only one species—bread alone. The chalice was reserved for those who were ordained.

Other customs sprang up. Part of a consecrated host was saved from one Mass for the next, to show all Masses were a single act. The reserved host was kept in a cupboard near the altar or in a container suspended from the ceiling—early tabernacles—and the people bowed toward it in respect. In the eleventh century, a flare-up in a controversy over the Real Presence of Christ in the Eucharist led to genuflecting, to demonstrate even more respect. One hundred years later a lighted candle began to be kept before the tabernacle. A century after that, the priest began to elevate the host during the consecration.

Also about this time, reception of the Eucharist dropped and devotion to Jesus in the Blessed Sacrament increased. Taking Communion would reach such a low point the bishops and councils would urge the laity to receive at least one time a year—the so-called "Easter duty." (It would remain as one of six "laws of the Church.")

The feast of Corpus Christi—the Body of Christ—was introduced in France in 1246 and to the rest of the Church less than two decades later.

Processions, with the Eucharist being displayed in an ornate container called a monstrance, became popular. Sometimes these were attached to the Mass, and sometimes even came to assume more importance than the Mass itself. Processions led to Benediction, reverencing the Blessed Sacrament at a special service. (At Benediction the consecrated host is put in a monstrance, placed on an altar with lighted candles, and incensed. This is followed by silent prayer, hymns and Scripture readings. Then the priest uses the monstrance to bless the people. The service concludes with the litany known as the Divine Praises.)

For many people, the Mass took a back seat. And abuses were not uncommon. A priest would say a "votive Mass" for a particular intention for a stipend, for money. To some, it seemed that the Mass was for sale. Martin Luther—and others—said the Catholic Church was getting off track. And because of some of the church's excesses they weren't entirely wrong.

Q. & A:
How Did the Mass Get Its Name?

When did Christians start using the word "Mass"?
That—or, really, its Latin equivalent—has been the common term since the fourth century.

What was used before then?
"The Lord's Supper" was first. And the "Eucharist."

What does "Eucharist" mean?
When we say that now we mean the Mass or Holy Communion, the bread and wine transformed into Christ's Body and Blood. But the word itself comes from the Greek word for *thanksgiving*.

The Mass is the ultimate prayer of thanksgiving.

What about "liturgy"?
That comes from the Greek for a public duty or work, and referred to Christ's saving work for us. It was used in both the East and West until "Mass" became more common in the West.

So where did "Mass" come from?
From *"missa,"* meaning sent. Since only the baptized could take part in the Liturgy of the Eucharist, at the end of the Liturgy of the Word the catechumens—those preparing for baptism—were sent away. And, at the end of the Liturgy of the Eucharist, the baptized were likewise sent forth with the Latin command, *"Ite missa est"* or "Go, you are sent."

(Those parts were called the Mass of the Catechumens and the Mass of the Faithful.)

Even today, the Mass ends with the sending "Go in peace."

At first *"missa"* only referred to those two dismissals but, over time, it became the word for the entire ceremony.

Justin Martyr on the Mass

In his "First Apology," first-century writer St. Justin Martyr described early Eucharistic celebrations this way:

And on the day called Sunday, all who live in cities or in the country gather together to one place, and the memoirs of the apostles or the writings of the prophets are read, as long as time permits; then, when the reader has ceased, the president verbally instructs, and exhorts to the imitation of these good things.

Then we all rise together and pray, and, as we before said, when our prayer is ended, bread and wine and water are brought, and the president in like manner offers prayers and thanksgivings, according to his ability, and the people assent, saying Amen; and there is a distribution to each, and a participation of that over which thanks have been given, and to those who are absent a portion is sent by the deacons.

And they who are well-to-do, and willing, give what each thinks fit; and what is collected is deposited with the president, who helps the orphans and widows and those who, through sickness or any other cause, are in want, and those who are in bonds and the strangers sojourning among us, and in a word takes care of all who are in need.

But Sunday is the day on which we all hold our common assembly, because it is the first day on which God, having wrought a change in the darkness and matter, made the world; and Jesus Christ our Savior on the same day rose from the dead. For He was crucified on the day before that of Saturn [Saturday]; and on the day after that of Saturn, which is the day of the Sun, having appeared to His apostles and disciples, He taught them these things, which we have submitted to you also for your consideration.

CHAPTER FOUR

The Council of Trent: Not Quite Carved in Stone

It would be hard to overemphasize the impact the Council of Trent had on the liturgy. It set the Tridentine Mass in place—some say it froze the Mass in place—for the next four centuries. (*Go to: Q. & A.: "What Happened at Trent?"*)

Priests in the early 1960s were strictly adhering to the words and actions that had been chosen four hundred years earlier. But, as the liturgical reformers of the mid-twentieth century noted, those words and actions didn't always necessarily accurately reflect what had occurred at the Last Supper or the Lord's Supper.

We need to be clear on this. The Mass, through it all, remained the Mass. Bread and wine were blessed and became the Body and Blood of Jesus. His followers, through it all, continued to "do this in memory of me."

The Council of Trent addressed a number of issues, including the Mass. But, likewise, there were a number of issues that prompted the calling of the council, all now falling under the general heading of the Reformation.

The Reformers—who would come be called "Protestants" (*Go to: "How the 'Reformers' Became the 'Protestants'"*)—were pointing out a number of failings within the institutional Church.

Martin Luther, the Augustinian monk who became the leader of the Protestants, had concerns about the Mass and the Eucharist.

Luther said the Catholic teaching on transubstantiation just didn't do the job. (That's the bread and wine becoming the Body and Blood of Christ.) He also believed the Mass was not a sacrifice. (That's a topic in chapter 6.)

But unlike other reformers, he *did* continue to believe in the Real Presence. That Jesus is there—Body and Blood, humanity and divinity—in the consecrated bread and wine. Among the others who said it just wasn't so was the Swiss theologian Huldrych Zwingli.

For a time, that became the hot topic. When Luther and Zwingli met to debate it in October 1529, the outcome was more than just a failure to reach an agreement. Here was proof that Protestantism itself was divided. In those "honeymoon" years of the early Reformation, some folks assumed as long as people of good will based their beliefs on Scripture, there could be only harmony.

This showed that wasn't the case.

But even though there wasn't total agreement among the reformers, their movement gained strength and popularity as it swept across Europe.

Just as in the early Church when the leaders had met in councils to deal with heresies, now they gathered to address the issues raised by the reformers. They began the "Counter-Reformation," a rather unfortunate name since before the Protestant Reformation, and during its rise, the Church had been attempting to reform itself. Respected Catholics were among those pointing out the Church's flaws.

At the Council of Trent the bishops were able to come up

with decrees that addressed a variety of issues, including many dealing with the Mass. They:

- approved of the term "transubstantiation" to define and explain what happens at the consecration;
- said the laity weren't to receive the Blood of Christ from the chalice;
- reaffirmed that the Mass had a sacrificial character;
- said the Mass was to be celebrated only in Latin. (A hotly debated topic. Some wanted the use of the vernacular.)
- reformed the missal, the book of Mass prayers.

Just as we live in the shadow of the Second Vatican Council, the late sixteenth century was a period when a council's decrees had to be interpreted and applied.

Because some of the impetus behind calling the council was reacting to what the Protestants were saying and doing, the fall-out was that the Catholic Reformers reinforced whatever the Reformers were taking issue with. How did the bishops do that? By reaffirming Catholic truths. The council wasn't simply a knee-jerk reaction but, at the same time, the bishops *did* need to more explicitly address areas of concern that Protestants were emphasizing.

Since the Protestants were criticizing Catholicism's devotion to the saints and praying to the Virgin Mary, Church leaders promoted these. Since they—or at least some of them—were saying Christ was not truly present in the Eucharist, the Church leaders pushed adoration of the Blessed Sacrament.

Since the Reformers pointed out that all baptized people share in Jesus' priesthood, the Church stressed the difference between the ordained and the laity.

And the Mass was one spot where a lot of that could be

emphasized. Where a lot of it could be experienced.

Now it was the priest who said Mass and the people who merely watched. This ritual—all of it in Latin and some of it whispered—was truly a mystery.

So what were members of the laity expected to do? Pray privately. Pray silently. The rosary was a good choice. Saying the rosary during Mass would be a practice that would continue up until the changes brought about by Vatican II. If not always actively promoted, it was certainly commonly accepted.

Missals—personal prayer books which included the prayers of the Mass—weren't allowed for the laity at first. A century later, the regulation became even stricter. It was forbidden to translate the Roman Latin missal into the vernacular.

It wouldn't be until the end of the nineteenth century—in 1897—that missals in the vernacular appeared in Europe, and not until 1927 in the United States. (The first was the St. Andrew's Daily Missal, published in St. Paul, Minnesota.) Up until then, the faithful could have prayer books in their native language but not missals.

The use of personal missals jumped dramatically during World War II when an American priest came up with a pocket-size edition for folks in the military. Service men and women used the little books worldwide and the practice became common in the United States. It was part of the beginning of the laity's active participation in the Mass.

Devotion to the Blessed Sacrament

After Trent it became more common for Catholics to receive Communion at Mass, but it wasn't always considered an integral part of going to Mass. Reception of the Eucharist at Mass, we might say, was above and beyond the call of duty ... or worthiness. Historians say that, with the Mass and Communion separated, it became more common to receive after Mass or even outside of Mass.

They also point out that, at the same time, there was a deep, popular devotion to Our Lord in the Eucharist, meaning the consecrated host. The tabernacle, the box that held the Blessed Sacrament, was placed at the center of the altar or just above the altar and became the centerpiece and focal point in churches. Making visits to Our Lord in the Eucharist was seen as a form of devotion that vied with (if not actually surpassed) going to Mass.

Now many came to regard a church as "God's house," the building in which Christ was kept in the tabernacle, more than the place where the faithful—priest and people alike—gathered for the "breaking of the bread" in memory of the One who had died to save them.

The Mass, still central to Catholicism, lost popularity to Benediction and Forty Hours Devotion, ceremonies paying particular honor to the Blessed Sacrament. This isn't meant to imply there's something wrong with or bad about devotion to the Eucharist, then or now. Perpetual adoration, for example, is a tremendous blessing for a parish. The concern is when that devotion eclipses the basic and supreme role of the Mass.

Seeds of Change

There's one final point that needs to be made. The changes brought about by Vatican II (and we'll look at those in the next chapter) didn't just come out of nowhere. It's more accurate to say the Mass was *largely* set in place by the Council of Trent but not entirely.

Liturgists say the changes in the second half of the twentieth century can be traced back to the nineteenth. The country whose government had adored the goddess Reason was also the one that first began to examine the liturgy and consider how and why Catholics were worshiping in a particular manner.

It was the Benedictine monks in Solesmes, France, who sparked the interest of others. One way they did this was restoring Gregorian chant, the "plainsong" that had its roots in early medieval times (and still could make a best-selling compact disc in the 1990s).

Pope St. Pius X (1903–1914) gave his nod of approval to their work and encouraged liturgical study and development.

He's also the pontiff who changed a longstanding tradition when it came to First Holy Communion. For centuries, children didn't receive Our Lord in the Eucharist. That privilege was reserved until one was a teenager. St. Pius X dropped the age limit down to what is known as the "age of reason" (not to be confused with the Age of Reason) – meaning when a child can easily determine right from wrong.

He also encouraged Catholics to received Communion frequently. And he appointed a committee to look into possible revisions in the Mass.

The "liturgical movement" puttered along during the 1920s and 1930s but didn't get very far. It was during and after World War II that the pace picked up.

Pius XII (1939–1958) took the next steps with a series of encyclicals—letters—titled "Mystical Body" (1943), "Sacred Liturgy" (1947) and "On Sacred Music" (1955).

The decade leading up to Vatican II saw a number of changes:

- The Rites of Holy Week were revised in 1956. (Holy Week, from Palm—or Passion—Sunday until Easter has a number of particular liturgies.)
- The fasting that was mandatory before receiving the Eucharist was also changed. The rule had been nothing to eat or drink from midnight on. Later it changed to three hours for food and one hour for drink. And, finally, one hour for both.
- Permission was also first granted to allow afternoon and evening Masses.
- The "dialogue Mass" was introduced in 1958. For the first time in centuries, the people were speaking aloud, actively responding to the celebrant.
- The vernacular was allowed in the administration of the sacraments.
- And, finally, in 1962 a seven-step program for the baptism of adults was approved.

But all that would pale—it would seem minor—in comparison to what lay in store with Vatican II. The changes that would come so quickly truly were unimaginable to most Catholics at the time. Now there is a generation that has known nothing but the Mass as it's experienced today.

Q. & A.:
What Happened at Trent?

Why was the council held in Trent?
It's a more central location than Rome, located along a historic route through Brennar Pass between Austria and Italy.

So it's Italian?
Now it is. Since the third century B.C., it's been controlled by the Romans, the Ostrogoths, the Lombards, the Franks, the Germans, the Austrians and the French.

Why is the Mass associated with the council called "Tridentine?"
That means "Trent-en." (Just like something from Naples in Neapolitan.) The ancient name for the city was Tridentum.

Did the council really last eighteen years?
Yes. And no. It began in 1545 and ended in 1563 but wasn't running continuously. There were three periods:

- 1545–47: The bishops addressed the central doctrinal issues raised by the Protestants. The council said Scripture had to be understood with the tradition (the teaching) of the Church, not "Scripture alone." The Council Fathers also answered the Protestant position on "justification" (on how God redeemed us and what our role in his plan is).
- 1551–52: This session looked at the sacraments.
- 1561–63: The final meetings dealt with disciplinary questions within the Church, including the obligation of a bishop to live within his own diocese. In 1564, Pope Pius IV published the "Profession of the Tridentine Faith" which summed up the council's decrees.

How many bishops attended the council?

The Council of Trent wasn't like Vatican II. Photographs from the Second Vatican Council show thousands of bishops from around the world packed into St. Peter's Basilica in Rome.

At the first session in Trent, there were thirty-one. None from Protestant territories. Most were Italian. In fact, Italians held the majority for all three sessions. The total number attending from '45 to '63 was 270. (Including 187 Italian, 31 Spanish, 26 French and 2 German.)

Was anyone else there?

Yes. Theologians and religious (members of orders) were also on hand.

Was that the Church's first council?

No. It was the nineteenth "ecumenical"—or universal—council. The first had been in Nicaea in 325. The most recent had been the Fifth Lateran, in Rome, from 1512 to 1517. It had been called to address the need of reform within the Church but failed in the attempt. It concluded before Luther posted his ninety-five theses in 1517.

Why did the Church wait another twenty-eight years before the next council?

Luther wanted one as early as 1520. So did leaders on both sides of the controversy. But the pope, Clement VII, was concerned that calling a council might give the impression that such a meeting had more authority than he did.

His successor, Paul III, was elected on what we might call a "platform" that included promising to call a council. He tried to do that two times before Trent.

Politics played a role, too. Lutheranism made things tough for Emperor Charles V of Germany and so other rulers, such as King Francis I of France, saw no reason to resolve the problem quickly. And politics, at this time, had much to do with conquering land and people. Charles V sacked Rome in 1527.

How the "Reformers" Became the "Protestants"

Historians point out that Protestantism owes its success, in part, to the Turks. And it's how the movement, and its followers, got their names.

That's because:

a. After Luther was excommunicated in 1521, he was banned in the German empire by Charles V.

b. Charles V was usually out of the country. (Out sacking Rome, for example.)

c. He was on the road so much, a temporary "truce" between Catholics and "Lutherans" became the status quo.

d. When Charles V did get back home, he met with his princes in 1529 but he still wasn't ready to solve the problem and he had bigger concerns, particularly Moslims (Turks) who were invading the eastern parts of his empire.

e. That meant Charles needed as many friends as possible among the princes, including those who backed Luther.

f. At the 1529 meeting, Charles asked for the princes'

help against the invaders on the eastern front and requested "that, at home on the religious front, life return to the way it had been before Luther ... until a general Church council could be called to address the issues being raised.

g. The Lutheran princes protested against Charles' second request, the first "Protestants."

CHAPTER FIVE

The Words We Pray
Show What We Believe

Non-Catholics attending a Mass for the first time can be amazed at how complicated the service seems. Even more perplexing is how the community knows when to sit, stand or kneel.

Is Father flashing hand signals that the visitor just isn't catching? Is a light blinking, a soft buzzer sounding?

After being at a Mass a few times, the postures of prayer seem so natural it's possible to shift from one to another with hardly a notice.

In this chapter we're going to look at a couple of things. A general outline of the Mass as it's celebrated now, and the origins and purposes of those particular prayers or actions.

Since the Second Vatican Council there is more flexibility in how a priest is allowed to celebrate Mass. Prior to that, from the Council of Trent in the sixteenth century up until the 1960s, a Roman Catholic Mass in Rome in 1600 would be nearly identical to a Mass in Paris in 1700 to a Mass in New York in 1800 to a Mass in Manila in 1900.

It might be a "high Mass" (one that also featured a deacon, subdeacon, a choir, several servers, incense and quite a few candles) or a "low Mass" (one that was much simpler) but the Latin text was the same. In the first half of the twentieth century,   a

typical U.S. parish would have one high Mass on Sunday and several low Masses. Some parishioners chose the high because of the music and ceremony. Others preferred the low because it was "quiet" and—truth be told—because it was always shorter.

As we mentioned before, at either celebration, members of the congregation could be more spectator than participant. Yes, they prayed but it wasn't necessarily the same prayer the priest was saying. Many silently recited rosaries throughout the liturgy. Others followed along in their missals.

In a sense, the liturgical changes following Vatican II loosened up the Mass by making more options available to the celebrant. A priest and parish could make some choices that better met the needs of the local community. So now a Mass celebrated in Lagos, Nigeria, won't necessarily perfectly match one in Lima, Peru.

Even so, the basics—worldwide—are the same. It isn't "anything goes." We'll say that again. The basics are the same. That's what we'll look at now.

Introductory Rites

Entrance Song

The introductory rites begin with the entrance song. The people stand as the celebrant enters and they either sing a song or say the "antiphon"—the entrance prayer—for that day.

The priest goes up to the altar and kisses it, as a sign of reverence to this symbol of Christ.

Sign of the Cross

He then leads the people in the Sign of the Cross. They respond "Amen."

This gesture is done by taking the right hand and touching it to the forehead, chest, left shoulder and right shoulder, while saying, "In the name of the Father and of the Son and of the Holy Spirit. Amen."

The sign of the cross demonstrates that we Catholics believe in the "Trinity," three persons in one God. And it says we believe we have been saved by Christ, who died on the cross.

The words can be found at the end of Matthew's Gospel (28:19) where Jesus says, "Go therefore and make disciples of all nations, baptizing them in the name of the Father and of the Son and of the Holy Spirit."

In the early third century, the theologian Tertullian noted that Christians used it often. "In all the actions of everyday life, we trace the sign of the cross."

(Why do Roman Catholics and Orthodox Christians use different shoulders first? The Orthodox follow the more ancient tradition. The Roman Catholics switched to better mirror the priest giving the blessing.)

Greeting

Next the celebrant greets the people, usually using a particular passage from the New Testament: "The grace of the Lord Jesus Christ, the love of God, and the fellowship of the Holy Spirit be with you all" (2 Cor 13:13). Or: "Grace to you and peace from God our Father and the Lord Jesus Christ" (Rom 1:7, Phil 1:2). Or, simply, "The Lord be with you."

The people answer, "And also with you."

Penitential Rite

At Sunday Mass, the priest can then bless some water and sprinkle it on the people as they sing an appropriate song. This reminds the congregation of their baptism and is a symbol of cleansing and healing.

More typically, the priest invites the people to "call to mind" their sins in silence and to ask God's forgiveness. Then, together, they recite the Confiteor. (Many of the prayers retain their Latin names.) This prayer begins "I confess to almighty God, and to you, my brothers and sisters, that I have sinned through my own fault."

In the old Latin prayer it was "mea culpa, mea culpa, mea maxima culpa." That is "through my fault, through my fault, through my most grievous [or biggest] fault." The person reciting the prayer would strike his or her breast with each phrase, a token form of penance. These days, missals note "they strike their breast" but that custom is becoming less common.

The Confiteor is a beautiful prayer. The person saying it goes on to confess he or she has erred "in my thoughts and in my words, in what I have done and in what I have failed to do."

It continues, "And I ask blessed Mary, ever virgin, all the angels and saints, and you, my brothers and sisters, to pray for me to the Lord our God."

So one of the first prayers of the Mass has a person standing side by side with his or her neighbors and saying, "I did wrong. Please pray for me."

The priest then responds, "May almighty God have mercy on us, forgive us our sins and bring us to everlasting life." And the people say "Amen."

In place of, or in addition to, the Confiteor, the priest can lead the people in the Kyrie (pronounced KEER-ee-ay). This prayer gets it name from the Greek. Even when the Mass was said in Latin, this prayer was recited in Greek.

The priest can provide his own "invocation," his own prayer, and then say "Lord, have mercy." The people answer with those same words. Then another prayer and "Christ, have mercy." And again, the people answer that way. And then a third brief prayer and "Lord, have mercy" with the same response.

The Kyrie is another ancient prayer, going back to the fourth century.

Gloria

This hymn of praise uses words found in the Gospel of Luke, chapter 2. On the night Jesus is born, the angels say, "Glory to God in the highest and peace to his people on earth."

The Gloria has been around since at least the fourth century. First it was used only at Christmas midnight Mass when it was sung by the bishop. In the fifth century it began to be used at Sunday Masses and on big feast days. That's the way it is now, too.

The Gloria isn't prayed during Advent or Lent. And at the Easter Vigil Mass it's really belted out, usually with bells ringing during the whole song.

Opening Prayer

The opening prayer is recited by the priest. He stretches out his arms to symbolize the new person now freed by the Resurrection and says, "Let us pray." After a moment of silence he reads the prayer for that particular feast or Mass from the missal. The prayer reflects the liturgical season or event being celebrated.

In the past this was called the "collect." It's been a part of the liturgy since the fifth century. At one time it was the final prayer—the summing up—of a litany (a list) of prayers which the celebrant "collected."

The people answer "Amen."

The Liturgy of the Word

Now the congregation sits as God's words are read. As we talked about in chapter 2, the two great parts of the Mass—the Liturgy of the Word and the Liturgy of the Eucharist—weren't always celebrated at the same time. And, as we said, our use of readings and a sermon are based on the formula used in synagogues at the time of Christ.

Then and there it was two readings, a sermon and a prayer. It was at such a service that Jesus stood up in his own hometown and announced he was the anointed one—the Messiah—sent by God (see Lk 4:16-21).

Why are these Scripture readings so important to the Mass? Because, as the bishops pointed out in their *Constitution on the Sacred Liturgy,* a Vatican II document, Christ "is present in his Word, since it is he himself who speaks when holy Scriptures are read in church" (7).

The readings vary, but as a whole, are used to present the faith. On Sundays, this is done with a three-year cycle, referred to as years A, B, and C, based on the Gospels of Matthew, Mark and Luke.

The celebrants or congregations don't choose any of the Sunday Mass readings. That's already determined and applied universally. You'll hear the same passages whether you're attending Mass at a basilica in Rome or mission parish in the remotest diocese in the world.

Sunday Masses have two other readings. One from the Old Testament complements the Gospel reading for that day. And another is usually from an ongoing reading from a New Testament book that is not a Gospel.

During the liturgical seasons of Advent (leading up to Christmas) and Lent (leading up to Easter), all three readings have a single theme.

It's a little different with the readings for the other days of the week. Monday through Saturday is on a two-year cycle and those Masses have only two readings: an Old Testament or "non-Gospel" selection and one from the Gospels.

So a Sunday Mass goes like this:

First Reading

After the people and celebrant sit down, a lector steps up to the pulpit (the lectern) and reads the selection from the Old Testament.

This isn't considered "ancient history." Or shouldn't be. Rather, it's showing the congregation a basic theme from the time before Christ—creation, God as shepherd, the promise of the Messiah—which, listeners know, has been fulfilled in some way in Jesus. The Church is saying we can't understand the Good News of the New Testament—who Jesus is, what he did and what he continues to do—without knowing the Old.

At the end of the reading, the lector says, "The Word of the Lord." And the people answer, "Thanks be to God."

Responsorial Psalm

This is a transition between the first two readings. It's a synagogue custom from the time of Christ. It gives the congregation a moment to pause and reflect on what was just read. This can be an excerpt from a Psalm, with the people reciting a refrain between verses, or, as was done in first-century Judaism, it can be sung.

This prayer has also been known as the "gradual."

Second Reading

From Trent to Vatican II, there were only two readings. The first was known as the epistle—coming from the Greek word for "letter." Often the first reading was from one of the letters of the New Testament.

The epistles often speak to congregations today because they were written (by Paul and others) to particular first-century communities. To the people of Rome. Of Corinth. Of Galatia. And so on. Each group had its strengths and its weaknesses. Just like communities today.

Sometimes the selection deals with Christian living. Sometimes it's a note saying the author wishes he was back with that group. Sometimes it's taking the people to task for not being the community they are called to be.

Again, the reading ends with the lector saying, "The Word of the Lord," and the people responding, "Thanks be to God."

Alleluia or Gospel Acclamation

Now the people stand up as the celebrant (or the priest or deacon who is going to give the homily) moves to the pulpit. There is a small procession with the celebrant carrying the lectionary and the altar servers carrying lighted candles. Once at the pulpit, the celebrant may incense the book.

This short prayer has been a part of the Mass since the fourth century. At first it was said only during the Easter liturgy but Pope St. Gregory the Great (590–604) allowed it to be a part of every Mass all year long, except during Advent and Lent.

The priest, deacon—or more usually, a cantor—says or sings "alleluia" and the people answer the same way. Then the priest or cantor reads a short sentence that ties in with the readings and everyone says "alleluia" again.

"Alleluia" comes from the Hebrew for "Glory to Him, who is, praise God."

Lent and Advent are the exceptions. Those two penitential times skip the "alleluia" and substitute the phrase "Praise to you, Lord Jesus Christ, king of endless glory" And on Easter and Pentecost a special poem or song is used here to get the congregation ready for the Gospel reading. It's called a sequence.

Gospel

Since the fourth century, it's been only the bishop, priest or deacon who reads the Gospel at Mass.

Again there is a dialogue. "The Lord be with you." "And also with you." "A reading from the holy Gospel according to ..." And the evangelist is named. "Glory to you, Lord."

Here it is customary to use the right thumb to make the sign of the cross on one's forehead, lips and heart. Often the action is accompanied by the silent prayer that the Lord be on the person's mind (thinking about God), tongue (talking about God) and heart (loving God). It says that Jesus' words—heard, spoken and taken to heart—are the source of our faith.

The priest or deacon offers a prayer that God will "cleanse my heart and my lips that I may worthily proclaim your Gospel."

At the end of the reading he concludes with, "The Gospel of the Lord." The people answer, "Praise to you, Lord Jesus Christ." Then he kisses the book as a sign of reverence.

Homily

Now the people sit for the homily. In our time, a homily is based on the Scriptures of the day, the particular feast being celebrated, the liturgical season or a part of the liturgy itself. Why a homily at this point? Because the first Christians weren't creating something from scratch. Many were strong, faith-filled Jews and they used the formula or agenda with which they were familiar.

Which, it seems safe to speculate, they liked and found worthwhile.

The Church recommends a homily be given. Why? Because it can help people apply what the readings have said. Or it can help them look at another issue that is important to the community right then.

Profession of Faith

After the homily, the priest returns to the altar and invites the people to stand and profess their faith. This could be the Nicene Creed, the Apostles' Creed or (if there's also a baptism during the Mass) the renewal of baptismal vows.

As we mentioned before, in the early Church, the catechumens—those preparing for baptism—left before the profession of faith. Today, with the Rite of Christian Initiation of Adults, those preparing for baptism and those preparing to "make a profession of faith" (people already baptized but not Catholic) at the Easter vigil leave before the recitation of the Creed. They head off with their teachers to do some studying, discussing and reflecting.

Weekday Masses don't include a profession of faith.

General Intercessions, the Prayers of the Faithful

The congregation continues to stand as the lector or celebrant reads special prayers composed for that community (for particular intentions, for sick or recently deceased members, and so on). Again, this has Jewish roots but for a long time it wasn't used except on Good Friday.

Today a typical formula is:

"For ... We pray to the Lord."

And the people answer, "Lord, hear our prayer."

Sometimes the members of the congregation are invited to add their own petitions out loud. Or to say them silently.

At the end of the list, the celebrant finishes with a prayer.

This concludes the Liturgy of the Word.

The Liturgy of the Eucharist

Collection

The people sit once again and, at Sunday Masses at most parishes, a collection is taken up after the Prayers of the Faithful. These contributions pay the community's bills and give it a fund to offer help to others. It's also an opportunity for people to practice the biblical call to tithe. We get that word from the Greek for "tenth." It's the Lord's invitation to us to be good stewards and give back the firstfruits of what we have to be used for the works of his kingdom.

The collection isn't an "official" part of the Mass like the readings or prayers, although even from early times, people brought gifts to the altar.

Preparation of Gifts

It has become customary now—again, we're talking about Sunday Masses—to have a couple of parishioners bring up the gifts to the priest. That means some unconsecrated hosts and the wine and water.

By the third century the offertory procession was part of the liturgy. Over time, gifts, not limited to money, but including food and such, were brought up to be given to the poor later. But as the Mass became less like a community meal, that faded. Vatican II reinstated the procession.

As the Roman Missal explains, "The rite of carrying up the gifts continues the spiritual value and meaning of the ancient custom when the people brought bread and wine for the liturgy from their homes."

Prayer Over the Bread and the Wine and Water

The priest takes the gifts and returns to the altar where he says a prayer over both the bread and the wine and water. His words "Blessed are you, Lord, God of all creation…" hearken back to the Passover meal.

At the end of both, the people respond, "Blessed be God forever."

If the congregation is singing during the Preparation of Gifts, the priest says the prayers quietly by himself.

Commingling the Water and Wine

Why water and wine? Before he prays over the wine, the priest puts a drop of water into it and says: "By the mystery of this water and wine may we come to share in the divinity of Christ, who humbled himself to share in our humanity."

In the Eastern Church, this is seen as a symbol of Christ's

humanity (the water) and his divinity (the wine). In the Church in the West, it represents the union of Christ (the wine) and his Church (the water).

This prayer was part of a longer one used at Christmastime about one thousand years ago.

Washing of the Hands

The altar servers or acolytes step forward at this point and pour a bit of water over the priest's hands (catching it in a small dish or bowl below his hands). Then they offer him a towel, which might be more like a cloth napkin.

As he washes his hands, the priest prays, "Lord, wash away my iniquity, cleanse me from my sins."

In the early Church this was more than symbolic. The priest was accepting gifts that weren't as clean as wine and hosts. Often he really did need to wash up.

An Invitation to Pray and a Prayer Over the Gifts

Next the priest invites the people to pray that "our sacrifice may be acceptable to God, the almighty Father." They answer, "May the Lord accept the sacrifice at your hands for the praise and glory of his name, for our good, and the good of all his Church."

The congregation now stands as the celebrant offers a brief prayer that, in the past, was called the "Secret" because he said it quietly, to symbolize that the Mass was holy and mysterious. While, obviously, it still is holy and still is a mystery, the community aspect of the liturgy is emphasized now so a secret prayer or one to be recited secretly would be inappropriate.

This ends the preparations.

The Eucharistic Prayer

There are a number of different Eucharistic Prayers the celebrant can use during this solemn part of the celebration when the bread and wine are consecrated, when they become the Body and Blood of Jesus.

Eucharistic Prayer I: This prayer (the longest of the Eucharistic prayers) goes back to the fourth century. It's called the Roman Canon and it points out the reason for the Mass: praising and thanking God the Father through his Son Jesus.

Eucharistic Prayer II: This is the oldest (and shortest) one, based on the writing of St. Hippolytus (c. 170-236).

Eucharistic Prayer III: This is, perhaps, the one most often used at parish Masses. It's based on a combination of liturgies from the East and West.

Eucharistic Prayer IV: Telling the history of salvation, this prayer is the one most based in Scripture.

Others: There are other Eucharistic Prayers with particular themes, including Masses of Reconciliation and Masses with Children.

Preface

This section of the Mass begins with a Preface, which starts with a dialogue between the celebrant and the people, who now stand.

"The Lord be with you." "And also with you."

"Lift up your hearts." "We lift them up to the Lord."

"Let us give thanks to the Lord our God." "It is right to give him thanks and praise."

That exchange, like so much of the Mass, has Jewish roots. It's similar to the formula used to invite and greet people in prayers of thanksgiving after a meal.

And then the priest offers another prayer that points out why thanks should be given, why the people gathered there should do that. The prayer varies, depending on the liturgical season and what feast day is being celebrated. It's an adaptation from the Book of Isaiah and from Psalm 117 (which begins, "Praise the Lord, all you nations. Extol him, all you peoples!").

The Preface concludes with the Sanctus, said by both the celebrant and the people. "Holy, holy, holy, Lord, God of power and might. Heaven and earth are full of your glory. Hosanna in the highest. Blessed is he who comes in the name of the Lord. Hosanna in the highest."

"Hosanna" comes from the Hebrew for "O Lord, save us, we pray."

Epiclesis

Generally, at this point the congregation kneels, although that's a custom that's been changing.

As the priest begins speaking, he puts his hands together and holds them over the bread and wine, praying an epiclesis prayer (coming from the Greek for "to call down"). He asks the Father to let the Spirit "come down upon these gifts to make them holy so that they may become for us the Body and Blood of our Lord Jesus Christ."

Later, there will be a second epiclesis, asking God to unite the people at the liturgy.

Consecration or Institution Narrative

The priest's prayer recalls what happened at the Last Supper when Christ instituted the Eucharist.

With the priest's words of consecration—echoing the words Jesus used on that night—the bread and wine become the Body and Blood of Christ. He elevates the bread and the chalice after he speaks each time.

There was a practical reason for this. In large medieval churches, with the priest facing the wall and the people at his back, the congregation couldn't see what was happening on the altar. Raising the host—a large one that was easier to spot—and the chalice solved that problem.

The tradition of ringing a bell at that time also brought back the attention of anyone whose mind had wandered. Or who was deep in personal prayer. That's no longer the case now with the Mass in the vernacular and modern-day sound systems.

Acclamation of Faith

After the consecration, the celebrant asks the people to "proclaim our faith."

There are a couple of different responses that can be used here. The most common is, "Christ has died. Christ is risen. Christ will come again." Making a profession like that was a practice in the Eastern Church and in the early liturgies. But the custom fell out of popularity during the Middle Ages. It was reintroduced after the Second Vatican Council to, again, drive home the point that members of the congregation aren't an audience. They are to be taking part in the celebration.

Anamnesis and Offering

Next comes an anamnesis prayer (from the Greek for "calling to mind"). It is the people remembering what Jesus has done for them and giving thanks.

The Offering asks God to "look upon this sacrifice" and accept it.

Memorial Intercessions

Next there are prayers for the pope, the local bishop and bishops and clergy everywhere. For those at the Mass and for all God's people. For "all who seek you with a sincere heart."

The dead are prayed for and, finally, the people pray that they themselves, "your children," may "enter into our heavenly inheritance" with Mary, the apostles and the saints.

It's there, the prayer continues, that "freed from the corruption of sin and death, we shall sing your glory through Christ our Lord, through whom you give us everything that is good."

Doxology

The doxology (from the Greek for "glory") is a hymn praising God. The celebrant prays: "Through him [that is, Jesus], with him, in him, in the unity of the Holy Spirit, all glory and honor is yours, almighty Father, for ever and ever."

As he says or sings this, he holds up the host and chalice because everything is lifted up and made holy in Jesus.

The people answer, "Amen." This is known as the Great Amen. It is the end of the Eucharistic Prayer.

Communion Rite

If the people have been kneeling, they now stand.

The Lord's Prayer

Together the celebrant and people "pray with confidence to the Father in the words our Savior gave us."

The Our Father comes from Matthew 6:9-13. It's Jesus' response when the disciples ask him to teach them how to pray.

After the Our Father, there's a sequel called the embolism

(from the Greek for "to throw in"). It means an insertion or addition. This prayer amplifies the final petition in the Our Father.

"Deliver us, Lord, from every evil, and grant us peace in our day," it begins. "In your mercy keep us free from sin and protect us from all anxiety as we wait in joyful hope for the coming of our Savior, Jesus Christ."

Now the people recite a doxology that has been part of the Protestant version of the prayer for centuries: "For the kingdom, the power and the glory are yours, now and forever." (*Go to: Q. & A.: "Why Are There Two 'Our Fathers'?"*)

The Sign of Peace

Since apostolic times, Christians have greeted one another with a sign of Christ's peace. Examples are given both in the New Testament and in the writings of the early Church Fathers.

Pope Innocent I (401-417) decided this exchange would take place after the Eucharistic Prayer. A variation was used in the thirteenth century, when a sacramental—a crucifix, cross or some other holy item—was kissed by the people. Over time, the exchange became limited to just the ordained, but the revisions after Vatican II restored the original practice.

So now, as the Roman Missal explains, "Before they share in the same bread, the people express their love for one another and beg for peace and unity in the Church and with all mankind."

Fraction Rite

Every Mass still includes the breaking of the bread although this has changed since the first century. At that time, in a Jewish household, the father would begin a family meal by breaking apart a loaf of bread and sharing it with the others at the table. Jesus broke bread and shared it when he multiplied the loaves and fishes to feed the thousands who came to hear him and be healed by him (see Lk 9:16-17).

And, certainly, he broke the bread at the Last Supper. After his Resurrection, when visiting with two people on the road to Emmaus, Jesus is recognized by the pair "in the breaking of the bread" (Lk 24:13-35).

Again, over time, the unleavened bread used at the Passover became the wafers now commonly used at Mass. Even so, at every Mass just after the Sign of Peace, the host is broken and a sliver is dropped into the chalice containing the consecrated wine.

Now it's commonly seen as a symbol of Jesus' body and blood being reunited after his Resurrection. But, historians say, that isn't how or why it began. (For the Jews, the separation of the flesh from the blood equaled death. And those two elements coming together equaled life. That's why this is seen as a sign of the Resurrection and of Jesus offering his life to us.)

This tradition traces its roots back to the early Church when the bishop was the typical celebrant for the Lord's Supper. A host from his Mass was taken by runners to the local Masses being celebrated by priests and was dropped into the chalice before Communion. This symbolized that all Masses were united to the bishop's. As the number of congregations grew and the distance between a community and a bishop became greater, this was no longer practical.

The fraction became the symbol of this.

Lamb of God

During the breaking of bread and the fraction, the people say or sing the Lamb of God (*Agnus Dei* in Latin). This prayer has been a part of the Mass since the seventh century. It refers to Christ as the Passover lamb. (We'll talk more about lambs and sacrifices in the next chapter.) It became customary, and still is in some places, for members of the congregation to strike their breasts with each of the three "Lamb of Gods," using the penitential gesture that's part of the Confiteor.

Communion

Now the priest holds up the host and says, "This is the Lamb of God who takes away the sins of the world. Happy are those who are called to his supper." And the people respond, "Lord, I am not worthy to receive you, but only say the word and I shall be healed."

The words of this prayer are strikingly similar to those used by a Roman soldier who asked Jesus to heal his servant (see Mt 8:5-13).

The celebrant then prays quietly and receives Communion.

As people come forward to receive Communion, the Eucharistic minister says "The Body of Christ" and the individual responds, "Amen" (meaning "Yes" or "I believe"). At some Masses, people also receive the Blood. The chalice is offered and the minister says, "The Blood of Christ." Again, the response is "Amen." (*Go to: "Why Can't Non-Catholics Receive Holy Communion?"*)

Receiving the host in the hand was the ordinary method for centuries in the early Church, but that changed over time and receiving on the tongue was considered proper. Again, with the changes after Vatican II, the original practice became an option.

After receiving the Body and Blood of Christ, each person returns to his or her pew for thanksgiving. Most commonly, this means kneeling.

After Communion, the celebrant cleans out the chalice and then sits. When he does, the congregation does, too.

Prayer After Communion

The Mass is almost over. Now there is final prayer by the celebrant. (And, if there are any announcements, this is when they take place.)

Blessing and Dismissal

The Mass concludes with the priest blessing the people with the Sign of the Cross and telling them to "Go in peace to love and serve the Lord." The response is "Thanks be to God."

Go out from here. You're sent. So this isn't like "The End" at the conclusion of a movie. It means the Mass *must be lived.* We'll look more closely at that in chapter 8.

? *Q. & A.: Why Are There Two "Our Fathers"?*

Why does the Our Father have a "Protestant" and a "Catholic" version?

What's known as the Protestant ending began to be used in the very early Church, most likely because it was a formula that had been common in Jewish worship for centuries.

Why?

At some point, scribes copying Scripture began adding it to Jesus' words in Matthew as a gloss—meaning an interpretation or pious note in the margin. Over time, many glosses ended up being in the text itself. This was the case when the King James version of the Bible was published in 1611.

That was the translation Protestantism used most for more than three hundred years. Because it had the gloss as part of the text, their Our Father included it.

Now Scripture scholars say it was an addition to Matthew and not part of the original. And Protestant Bibles published since the King James translation have removed it from the text.

Why Can't Non-Catholics Receive Holy Communion?

As the American bishops explain, "Because Catholics believe that the celebration of the Eucharist is a sign of the reality of the oneness of faith, life and worship, members of those churches with whom we are not yet fully united are ordinarily not admitted to Holy Communion."

They add: "Eucharistic sharing in exceptional circumstances by other Christians requires permission according to the directives of the diocesan bishop and the provisions of canon law."

And they say: "We also welcome to this celebration those who do not share our faith in Jesus Christ. While we cannot admit them to Holy Communion, we ask them to offer their prayers for the peace and the unity of the human family."

This can be an emotional issue for some people. It's not intended to be exclusionary but a call to commitment and conversion.

CHAPTER SIX

The Ultimate—
and Perfect—Sacrifice

It's a classic scene from a B movie. The leading lady, a virgin dressed in a flowing white gown, is about to be hurled into the fiery volcano by the primitive tribe. An offering—a sacrifice—must be made to appease the god. But, of course, just in time the leading man swoops in to save her.

What does such obvious Hollywood claptrap have to do with the Mass? It, too, is described as a *sacrifice* because … well, because that's what it is.

Maybe in the past when you've heard that term "the Holy Sacrifice of the Mass" you assumed it meant *you* were the one giving up something. You sacrificed to get there that Sunday morning, with your little children in tow. Or you sacrificed to get there on the only day of the week that, otherwise, you could have slept in. Or maybe it seemed that, as a teen, you made that sacrifice to appease the "local gods"—your parents.

But when the Church talks about the Sacrifice of the Mass, what it means is closer to that B movie than to the minor hassles a person may go through to get to church.

Does that surprise you?

The Mass *is* a sacrifice. Each Mass. Every Mass. Jesus is the victim being offered to God. And, complicating the matter even more, he's also the one doing the offering *and*, as God, the one to whom the sacrifice is being offered.

Anthropologists and historians say cultures around the world have developed religious practices that include sacrifices. What's involved? Something of value—grain, wine, oil, livestock, a person—is consecrated to the god. Then that something is consumed—by killing it, by burning it, by pouring it out.

Why do the people make such a sacrifice? For a number of reasons, the researchers say. It's done:

- as a gift to the deity, to the god;
- to demonstrate the proper reverence a master would rightfully demand from a servant;
- to make up for past offenses;
- to take part in a sacrificial banquet with the god;
- to take the life that was released from the victim (animal or human) and send it to the god who would then return it to the people.

Not every religion has had—or has—sacrifices. But many do. Vedism, which has its roots in India, has a proverb that says, "Sacrifice is the navel of the world." It's that former link, that reminder, of where we came from, of how we were created. As with many cultures, the Vedic idea of sacrifice developed over time. And in fact, historians say, another proverb shows how the idea of honoring the deity for honor's sake alone became more this-for-that: "Here is the butter, where are your gifts?"

We've done our part. You owe us.

In the western world, the Greeks were no strangers to sacrifices, both unbloody and bloody. Offering grain, fruit or butter; or a lamb or calf. The Greeks and other westerners didn't just use raw materials. Pastries and drinks were made and sacrificed.

Ancient Rome had a calendar that described how and when to sacrifice to the gods. And like Greece, Rome had a lot of them.

It's good to keep in mind that this was the world—the time and the general region—where God stepped into human history in a unique and particular way. Egyptians, Assyrians, Babylonians, Canaanites, everyone in the neighborhood had sacrifices. Each had its own style, belief and gods, but, in general, they were pretty much the same.

Here's something we can touch, taste, smell. We're offering it to our deity and destroying it so it belongs to him/her/it/them alone.

Enter Yahweh. Speaking to Abraham. What does the Almighty ask of him? He wants a sacrifice. In their old age, Abraham and Sarah have been given a son. Now God wants the lad killed.

"Take your son, your only son Isaac, whom you love, and go to the land of Moriah, and offer him there as a burnt offering on one of the mountains that I shall show you" (Gn 22:2).

Although it was breaking the old man's heart, he knew what to do. He knew the necessary steps. So did his son, Isaac.

"Hey, Dad, what are we going to use for the sacrifice?"

"Don't worry about it. God will provide."

God did, of course. He was only testing Abraham and so he sent an angel to stop the father just before he killed his boy. And the Lord had a ram stuck in some bushes that could be used instead.

There are a couple of things to consider here. First, human sacrifice was rare but not unheard of in that region at that time. Abraham didn't seem to have any fear of someone reporting him to Child Protective Services or of the cops tracking him down after he'd done the deed.

But—and this is important—Yahweh was saying he didn't want human sacrifices. That flew in the face of current practice.

The Lord was bringing the message to the people, his people, that he is the one and only God, and he was showing that the one and only God doesn't want humans sacrificed to him.

Sacrifices, yes. Humans as the offering, no.

Abraham and Isaac aren't the first instance of sacrifice in the Old Testament. That can be found earlier in the fourth chapter of Genesis. Another family. The first family. Two sons of Adam and Eve want to pay homage to God. Abel was a shepherd. Cain, a farmer. Cain offered some of his harvest, Abel some of his firstlings, his lambs. The "fat portions," we're told.

God accepted Abel's offering but not Cain's. Many biblical commentators explain that Abel apparently sacrificed the best he had while Cain presented less than Grade A produce. But the author of Genesis doesn't say exactly why one sacrifice was accepted but the other wasn't. Why "for Cain and his offering he [Yahweh] had no regard" (Gn 4:5).

Later, though, Scripture points out it isn't just what is offered but how it is offered. That doesn't mean following a particular ritual, but with the proper attitude. Scripture scholars say verses that refer to God wanting obedience, not burnt offerings and sacrifices (see 1 Sm 15:22 or Is 1:10-17, for example), don't mean Yahweh is opposed to those rituals. The Lord is telling the Israelites that obedience is more important than the sacrifices they offer.

Even so, over centuries, the Hebrews *did* develop particular rituals, with exact steps to be performed at exact times.

The Hebrew Ritual

What does all this have to do with the Mass? Again, these are Christianity's roots. Examining what happened way back then, and why it happened, can shed a new or different light on the celebration of Mass today.

Even the terms we use—the priest stands at the altar—are ones that would be familiar to a Jew born centuries before Christ. It was with the destruction of the Temple in A.D. 70 that both the priesthood and the altar—the rituals of sacrifice offered there—ended. (*Go to: Q. & A.: "What Was So Great About the Temple?"*) So at the time Jesus was born, sacrifice was common. More than merely expected, it was demanded by Mosaic law.

For a bloody sacrifice, the animal had to belong to the person making the offering and it had to be clean, that is, not an animal deemed unclean by the Law. Unclean animals included dogs, pigs and camels. Oxen, sheep and goats were clean. No runts allowed. The best was to be offered to Yahweh.

Doves were just about the only sort of bird that could be used. If a family was poor, turtle doves or young pigeons could be substituted for a larger animal. Our Feast of the Presentation, celebrated on February 2, commemorates the Holy Family doing just that. Luke 2:22-38 tells the story of how Mary and Joseph "offered a sacrifice according to what is stated in the law of the Lord" (v. 24).

There were also unbloody sacrifices. A food or drink was used. Toasted ears of corn or shelled grain, with oil and incense. The sweet-smelling smoke was a symbol of the person's prayer going up to God. We use it the same way in our liturgies today. Wheat flour and unleavened bread were also offered. So were "firstfruits" and wine.

In some instances, the material that wasn't burned completely was set aside for the priests who worked in the temple. They were allowed to eat it.

In our own time, making any kind of sacrifice like that may seem strange to Christians, but the idea of a bloody one is especially foreign. It's good to remember that the Hebrews weren't involved in some pagan ritual, although pagan religions performed similar acts. This was a way of praying to the God of Abraham, Isaac and Jacob.

So what was the procedure? When a bloody sacrifice was to be made:

1. The victim, the animal, was brought forward. It was led to the outer court of the temple (or in earlier times, of the tabernacle, the tent used for worship).

2. Hands were imposed on it, that is, rested on its head. This gesture meant the one making the sacrifice transferred his personal intention to the animal. What personal intention? It could be adoration, thanksgiving, petition or atonement. Atonement was a common and popular choice. Today those four categories effectively describe the different types of Christian prayer. If the sacrifice was being made for the whole community, the elders imposed their hands in the name of all the people. For a time, burnt offerings could be made at the temple even for Gentiles. The imposition of hands was typically preceded by a verbal confession of sins.

3. The animal was killed, usually by a deep cut to the throat, by the sacrificer. The priest handled this if doves were used. And later, when it came to slaying, skinning and dismembering large animals, this was done by the priests and Levites (members of the tribe of Levi who worked in the Temple and helped the priests).

4. Its blood was sprinkled. This was the key to the whole ritual. The Law said it could be performed only by a priest. If a layperson did it, the sacrifice was invalid. Why was the blood so important? And not just among the Hebrews but with other cultures, too? In the Old Testament, the blood is the life of the creature. It was sprinkled on the altar, thrown at its base or smeared on other parts of it. Getting the blood onto the altar, one way or another, was the symbolic act of offering the life of the animal to God. It wasn't the killing of the animal that really mattered. It was the blood on the altar, the offering of the life.

5. The animal, or parts of it, were burned.

Under the general heading of bloody offerings, there were a number of divisions. A burnt offering, a holocaust, consumed everything except the hip muscle and hide. It was the oldest and most frequently and most widely used. It was top of the list and showed a person's or community's complete submission to God.

There were also sin offerings and guilt offerings. The first had to do with absolving the person's sins, the second with making satisfaction for the injuries the sins had inflicted. The Law included regulations on what sins could and couldn't be forgiven. Some of these sacrifices were used to remedy legal uncleanness, such as purification after childbirth. Guilt offerings were used for sins that demanded restitution. Cheating a neighbor, for example.

There was a third class of bloody sacrifice known as the peace offering. These were given to show thanks or praise, to fulfill a vow or just as a voluntary offering.

Just a few more details on this and then we'll move on to the New Testament. They have to do with peace offerings. First, this type included a special ceremony referred to as wave and heave. The breast and right shoulder of the animal were separated first.

In the wave, the priest placed the breast of the victim on the hands of the sacrificer and then placed his own hands under that person's hands. He then moved the hands and the breast backward and forward to symbolize the giving and receiving between God and the person.

In the heave, the right shoulder of the victim was used. This time the movement was up and down.

The breast and shoulder went to the priests, who were allowed to eat them. The rest of the animal was eaten by the offerer and his guests at a banquet in the sanctuary. Everything not eaten the first day was burned.

The peace offering was seen as presenting a banquet to God, who accepted it and then invited the worshipers to sit down at the meal with him. This was almost always a happy event.

In the New Testament

That was a lot of background. But it helps to know those things when looking at the Mass, when looking at what happened on Calvary.

The Book of Hebrews, chapter 9, explains that "Christ came as a high priest" (v. 11). It's hard for us not to think of a priest of today. But imagine a priest of the temple. Jesus didn't enter the temple or holy of holies, but heaven. And he didn't use "the blood of goats and calves, but ... his own blood, thus obtaining eternal redemption" (v. 12).

Why? Because "if the blood of goats and bulls, with the sprinkling of the ashes of a heifer, sanctifies those who have been defiled [by touching a corpse, for instance], how much more will the blood of Christ, who through the eternal Spirit offered himself without blemish to God, purify our conscience from dead works to worship the living God!" (vv. 13-14).

The author of Hebrews does a great job of capsulizing what has happened. This, he writes, is how our new relationship with God began. Jesus "is the mediator of the new covenant" (v. 15) that promises eternal life to humanity because "a death has occurred that redeems them from the transgressions under the first covenant" (v. 15).

What was the first one? The agreement between Yahweh and the Israelites led by Moses. Even that, Hebrews says, wasn't begun without blood. "For when every commandment had been told to all the people by Moses in accordance with the law, he took the blood of calves and goats, with water and scarlet wool and hyssop [a kind of plant], and sprinkled both the scroll itself and all the people, saying 'This is the blood of the covenant that God has ordained for you'" (vv. 19-20).

"Blood" and "covenant." Do the words sound familiar? They're used by Jesus at the Last Supper, at the first Mass. And they're used at the consecration of every Mass today.

The evangelists tell us that on the night before Jesus died, to quote Mark 14:22-24, "While they were eating, he took a loaf of bread, and after blessing it he broke it, gave it to them, and said, 'Take; this is my body.' Then he took a cup, and after giving thanks he gave it to them, and all of them drank from it. He said to them, 'This is my blood of the covenant, which is poured out for many.'"

Jesus—the perfect victim, completely unblemished—was going to be sacrificed. And unlike the sacrifices of the old covenant, this one had to be offered only one time because it was perfect (see Heb 9:25-28). It brought complete forgiveness and holiness (see Heb 10:5-18). After this sacrifice, Christians can "have confidence to enter the sanctuary by the blood of Jesus, by the new and living way that he opened for us through the curtain (that is, though his flesh)" (Heb 10:19-20).

In the Church

The early Church taught that the Eucharist was a true sacrifice with Jesus both the high priest and victim. That tradition was challenged in the sixteenth century by the Protestant Reformation. The Council of Trent clearly upheld: "Jesus Christ, a perfect priest, offered himself to God his Father on the altar of the cross, to bring about by his death eternal redemption." The first chapter on its decree on the Mass says Jesus left to his Church the visible, unbloody sacrifice that commemorates and perpetuates the sacrifice on the cross.

The Mass, the bishops wrote, is the "unbloody immolation of Christ." Only the manner of offering distinguishes it from the sacrifice on the cross. That's why the Mass has a propitiatory value, atoning for the sins of the living and the dead for which it is offered.

The Mass isn't a skit showing the Last Supper. It isn't a salute to the crucifixion. In his encyclical *Mediator Dei,* Pope Pius XII (1939-58) once again gave the Church's traditional teaching: "The Mass is a true sacrifice in which Christ, by an unbloody immolation, offers himself as a victim to God the Father as he had done on Good Friday."

The one making the offering is the same because the priest, the celebrant, has the power to perform this liturgical action *in persona Christi* (in the person of Christ). The Body and Blood of Christ are truly present in the Eucharist—under the appearance of bread and wine—while the unbloody immolation of Christ in the Mass is symbolized by the separation of the species.

The Mass doesn't repeat Calvary. Jesus died only one time. Once was enough. And it's not a simple remembrance of Calvary. It is a sacrament, instituted by Christ, who gave the apostles the matter and formula to be used.

To quote one Church document, the Mass is "a sacrifice in which the Sacrifice of the Cross is perpetuated" (from "Instruction on the Worship of the Eucharist," 1967).

The *Catechism of the Catholic Church* explains that when the Church celebrates the Eucharist, it commemorates Christ's Passover, and "it is made present: the sacrifice Christ offered once for all on the cross remains present" (*CCC* 1364) (cf. Heb 7:25-27).

Because it's the memorial of Christ's Passover, the Mass is also a sacrifice. In the Eucharist, Jesus gives us "the very body which he gave up for us on the cross, the very blood which he 'poured out for many for the forgiveness of sins'" (*CCC* 1365) (Mt 26:28).

"The Eucharist is thus a sacrifice because it re-presents (makes present) the sacrifice of the cross, because it is its memorial and because it applies its fruit" (*CCC* 1366).

Its fruit? The *Catechism* quotes from the Council of Trent to further explain that. Christ "wanted to leave to his beloved spouse the Church a visible sacrifice (as the nature of man demands) by which the bloody sacrifice which he was to accomplish once for all on the cross would be re-presented, its memory perpetuated until the end of the world, and its salutary [saving and healing] power be applied to the forgiveness of the sins we daily commit."[8]

Hang on. Just a couple more quotes. From the Catechism which again quotes Trent, noting that the sacrifice of Christ on the cross and the sacrifice of the Eucharist are *one single sacrifice:* "The victim is one and the same: the same now offers through the ministry of priests, who then offered himself on the cross; only the manner of offering is different."[9]

And we can join in the offering, that sacrifice. "The Church which is the Body of Christ participates in the offering of her Head. With him, she herself is offered whole and entire. She unites herself to his intercession with the Father for all.... In the Eucharist the sacrifice of Christ becomes also the sacrifice of the members of the Body. The lives of the faithful, their praise, sufferings, prayer, and work, are united with those of Christ and with his total offering, and so acquire a new value. Christ's sacrifice present on the altar makes it possible for all generations of Christians to be united with his offering" (*CCC* 1368).

Again, we don't have to be mere spectators at Mass. We aren't supposed to be. We can bring our own offering—our worries, our joys, our failings, our hearts and souls—to the altar and Christ will lift them up, with himself, to our heavenly Father, to the Creator of all things.

Q. & A.: What Was So Great About the Temple?

What was the temple?

A building that was *the* place of worship for the Jews from the time of Solomon (961–922 B.C.). During the Hebrews' early days—during the Exodus—a tent called a tabernacle, a movable shrine, was used.

What happened to the temple?

There have been three temples in Jerusalem, each on the same spot (where today the Harem-esh-Sharif—the Dome of the Rock, a Muslim shrine—stands). Part of the royal palace, the temple was more than simply a chapel.

The first, Solomon's, was destroyed by the Babylonians in 587 B.C. It was ninety feet long, thirty feet wide and forty-five feet high. It was a lavish affair and its center, its heart, was the Holy of Holies.

This inner sanctum was a cube, thirty feet on each side. Ordinary worshipers never entered it, only priests. And that was uncommon. Two cedar cherubim—angels—dominated the room. Each was fifteen feet high with a fifteen-foot wingspan. They stood over Israel's treasure: the ark of the covenant.

What was that?

The ark was small portable chest (about four feet by two feet by two feet) made of acacia wood with gold overlay inside and out. On top was a gold plate referred to as the mercy seat or place of atonement. It was the place where God accepted atonement.

On top were statues of two cherubim facing each other so that their wings overshadowed the seat. It was where "I [God] will meet with you [his Chosen People], and from above the mercy seat, from between the two cherubim that are on the ark of the covenant, I will deliver to you all my commands for the Israelites" (Ex 25:22).

The ark was thought to contain the two stone tablets of the Ten Commandments and was also traditionally believed to hold the rod of Aaron (the staff that had belonged to Moses' brother) and a container of manna (the bread provided to the Israelites in the desert). It went before the people as they traveled from Egypt and it led them into battle.

Needless to say, it had a long and colorful history, with tales of power that have come down to our own day—and "Indiana Jones."

Finally, it was placed in Solomon's temple (see 1 Kgs 8:6) and then it isn't mentioned again in the Old Testament historical books. Historians say it was destroyed, along with the temple, in 587 B.C.

How was the temple destroyed?
It was victim of war with the Babylonians.

Little is known about the second temple, dedicated in 515 B.C. and used until 19 B.C., when it was replaced by Herod's Temple. Historians say Herod built the place, over ten years, to make the Jews less hostile toward him.

They say he was more heathen than Jew. The interior decorating continued even longer.

This was the building referred to in the New Testament. Where the Holy Family visited and Mary and Joseph found their lost twelve-year-old, in his "Father's house." Where Jesus overturned the moneychangers' tables. Where he taught. Where, on Good Friday as Christ died, "the curtain of the temple was torn in two, from top to bottom" (Mk 15:38)—the veil separating the Holy of Holies. (Symbolically, the passage meant that now all people, not just the Chosen People, had access to God through Jesus' death.)

What happened to this temple?
It didn't last very long. Completed in A.D. 64, it was destroyed by the Romans in A.D. 70.

Why did the Romans destroy it?
The Romans were fighting a Hebrew uprising. They burned the building and tore it apart to punish the Israelites.

What does all this temple business have to do with Christians?
It helps to know what the temple meant to the Old Covenant because Jesus says he—his body, his Church—is the temple of the New Covenant.

He said, "Destroy this temple [meaning his body], and in three days I will raise it up" (Jn 2:19).

CHAPTER SEVEN

The Liturgical Year:
Every Day is Someone's Feast

We Catholics can say "Happy New Year" in late November or early December. That's because the Church doesn't follow a January-December calendar when it comes to the Mass.

The "liturgical" or "Church" year begins with the First Sunday of Advent and ends fifty-two weeks—minus one day—later on the Saturday after the Feast of Christ the King.

Obviously this schedule wasn't set up by Jesus at the Last Supper. It's one that developed over centuries. Now every Sunday is a particular feast, although some have only numbers "in Ordinary Time." (*Go to: Q. & A.: "Who Filled in the Church's Calendar?"*).

And every weekday can be a unique celebration, too, honoring a saint, Mary or an event in the life of Christ or the Church.

Just like the twelve months of the year can be divided into weather seasons (winter, spring, summer and fall) or sports seasons (basketball, baseball, football) or academic seasons (first semester, second semester, summer vacation), the Church year has seasons, too.

Why? Because, to quote the *Catechism of the Catholic Church,* "in the liturgical year the various aspects of the one Paschal [Easter] mystery unfold" (1171). The story of the Faith is told and taught, from the foretelling of the Messiah's coming centuries before the birth of Christ, to his Second Coming at the end of time.

This is how, annually, the Church does that.

Advent

Advent begins on the fourth Sunday before Christmas and ends on the day before Christmas. That means it can range from twenty-two to twenty-eight days. Christmas could be one day after the Fourth Sunday of Advent or one full week after it.

We get the word itself from the Latin *adventus,* meaning an arrival. In a non-religious context, it referred to an emperor's coming. In ancient times that was a momentous event. Roads, often lousy at best, really were made straighter and more direct when the emperor was coming to town. Potholes were filled in and bumps were leveled out.

Isaiah, the Old Testament prophet, uses that image when describing getting ready for the coming Messiah. Then valleys will be lifted up and mountains laid low (see Is 40:4). That same passage speaks of a voice crying out in the wilderness, getting the people ready for the Lord. In the New Testament, that voice is recognized as John the Baptist.

Isaiah and John—the last prophet—play prominent roles in the readings at Mass during Advent. ("Prophet" means someone who spoke God's truth. That might, or might not, include telling future events. It does mean that, too, for both these men.)

The Church says these four weeks have three purposes. One is to get people ready to commemorate Christ's birth. Which, as we all know, can sometimes be overlooked or given only a quick glance in the hustle and bustle of the holiday season. The second is to help them remember that Christ is coming again, not as a baby in a manger but as the final judge at the end of time. And the third reminds us of Christ's coming to each of us in our personal life.

Some historians say Christians began to mark Advent from the fourth century on but how it was celebrated varied from place to place. Rome used four weeks. Gaul, now France, liked a longer period.

The Roman practice, from the twelfth century, was codified by the Council of Trent. That meant the Church said "this is how we're all going to do it."

During Advent the priest wears purple vestments as a sign of penance. Rose is an option for the third Sunday, formerly called "Gaudete," meaning rejoice. (And also for the fourth Sunday of Lent, once known as "Laetare," also meaning rejoice.) Why rejoice? Because "rejoice" was the first word in the opening verse of the liturgy for these Sundays. And in the past it was a way of saying "Hang in there. Even in the middle of this time of penance there's reason to anticipate a celebration." (*Go to: "Vestments and Their Colors."*)

In the past, prior to the Code of Canon Law in 1917, adults were expected to fast during this time, just as during Lent. (*Go to: "Think Fast."*)

And like Lent, Advent Sunday Masses leave out the Gloria. That seems penitential but during these four weeks it's omitted so that it's even more impressive when it's used again on Christmas. It is, after all, based on the angels' words to the shepherds.

These days it's common for a parish to have an Advent

wreath lit during Mass. One candle marks each Sunday of the season. Many Catholics do the same at home. The traditional hymn while lighting the candles is "O Come, O Come, Emmanuel." The use of the wreath dates back to medieval times in northern Europe and is, historians say, a Christian practice replacing a pagan one.

Christmas Season

On the Church calendar, this season begins with the vigil of Christmas—prayers on Christmas Eve—and extends to the Sunday after January 6.

The Sunday after Christmas is the feast of the Holy Family. January 1 is the Solemnity of Mary. That's been in place since 1970. Prior to that, dating back to at least the first half of the sixth century, it was the Circumcision, marking Jesus' initiation into the Jewish faith eight days after his birth.

January 6 is the feast of Epiphany, the three wise men coming to visit the Christ Child and the manifestation of Christ to the world. It is the traditional twelfth day of Christmas. In the United States, Epiphany has now been moved to the nearest Sunday.

The Sunday after January 6 is the feast of the Baptism of the Lord, a day commemorating the beginning of Jesus' ministry to the people when he was about thirty.

Ordinary Time

Ordinary Time is the name given to the period between the Christmas season and Lent and between the Easter season and Advent. "Ordinary" doesn't mean common but "in order."

That is, each Sunday building on the previous one.

Its purpose is to examine the themes of salvation history—the story of how God stepped into history in a particular way with his Chosen People, the Israelites, and how Christ is the fulfillment of God's promise.

Lent

Lent starts on Ash Wednesday, sometime between February 4 and March 11, depending on when Easter occurs. It lasts until the Mass of the Lord's Supper on Holy Thursday. Historically, the season began as a period of preparing catechumens to be initiated into the Church at Easter. And it still serves that purpose today.

Ash Wednesday is a day of fast and abstinence. Adults can eat only two small meals and one main meal and must abstain from meat. Lenten Fridays are also meatless. In the not-too-distant past, all the days of Lent were fast days.

On Ash Wednesday the foreheads of the people are marked with ashes in the Sign of the Cross as the priest says, "Remember you are dust and to dust you shall return," or, "Turn away from sin and be faithful to the Gospel." Ash Wednesday isn't a holy day of obligation (we'll talk about those a little later), but many people come to Mass on that day.

The season of Lent has six Sundays. The last one was formerly known as Palm Sunday. Now it's called Passion Sunday. It's the first day of Holy Week. At many parishes, people pick up palms before that Mass, and the liturgy begins with a procession into church, symbolic of Christ's triumphal entry into Jerusalem those few days before he was killed.

In ancient times Lent was called *tessaracoste*—forty days—in

Greek. We get our name for it from the Middle English and Anglo-Saxon for "spring." Lent has always been seen as a time of fasting, special prayer and almsgiving (giving money or service to the needy) to get ready for the Church's great feast, Easter.

In the early centuries of the Church, Lent was a pre-Easter fast that lasted two or three days. Over time, it grew to three or four weeks.

We say Lent has forty days but it stretches over seven weeks. That's because, technically, the Sundays of the season aren't Lent. Forty has been the accepted number of days at least since the Council of Nicaea in 325. Historians say it's likely that figure was chosen because of Christ's forty days in the desert before his public ministry (which reflects Moses and the Israelites' forty-year journey from Egypt to the Promised Land).

During the third, fourth and fifth Sundays of Lent, there are scrutiny Masses for catechumens (who at that point are called the "elect") who will be received into the Church at the Easter Vigil. The scrutinies are a part of the Rite of Christian Initiation of Adults, which describes them as rites for self-searching and repentance rather than some sort of test. They have "above all, a spiritual purpose ... to uncover, then heal, all that is weak, defective or sinful in the hearts of the elect; to bring out, then strengthen, all that is upright, strong and good."

Easter Triduum

"Triduum" means three days. The Easter Triduum runs from evening Mass on Holy Thursday until Evening Prayer—Vespers—on Easter Sunday.

Holy Thursday commemorates the institution of the

Eucharist (the first Mass) and Holy Orders (the first priests). It's a special liturgy that includes a reenactment of Christ washing the feet of his apostles (see Jn 13). The main celebrant—whether a priest, bishop or pope—washes the feet of twelve people.

(Earlier that week there is a Mass of Chrism at which the bishop blesses the chrisms—the oils—used during the year for various anointings, such as the Sacrament of the Sick.)

After Mass on Holy Thursday evening, there is a procession to take the Blessed Sacrament to a place of repose where it can be adored by the people. This practice symbolizes watching and praying with Christ in the Garden of Gethsemane.

There is no "Mass" on Good Friday. The liturgy on this day includes the reading of the Passion according to John, special prayers for the Church and various groups of people, the veneration of the cross and a Communion service. This celebration usually takes place in the afternoon. Some parishes have services in the afternoon and in the evening.

On Holy Saturday there are no services. Mass isn't celebrated on this day. Holy Communion is given only as Viaticum. That means Communion given to a person who is near death.

The Easter Vigil Mass ("vigil" means celebrated on the evening or night before the feast) is the high point of the Church year. At that first Mass of Easter, a new fire is blessed and an Easter—or Paschal—candle is lit and used in a procession. The candle will be lit at Mass and morning and evening prayers throughout the Easter Season. The Mass includes the "Exsultet"—an Easter proclamation—and at least three Old Testament readings, the Litany of the Saints, the blessing of water, baptism of converts and the renewal of baptismal vows. There may also be confirmation and first communion.

It is *the* liturgy of the year.

Masses celebrated on Easter morning are much simpler than the vigil.

Easter Season

The Easter Season lasts fifty days, beginning on Easter and ending on Pentecost. Because Easter is a movable feast, so is Pentecost.

The weekdays after Easter Sunday are called Easter Monday through Easter Saturday. The Sundays that follow are numbered in relation to Easter, beginning with the Second Sunday of Easter and ending with the Seventh Sunday.

The Ascension—Christ's ascending into heaven—is celebrated on the Thursday of the sixth week, forty days after Easter. Historians says there's documentation of this feast being celebrated from the early fifth century but it's an event that was commemorated long before then in connection with Easter and Pentecost. After the Gospel on the Ascension, the Easter candle is extinguished and not used at Mass except for funerals and baptisms.

Pentecost is celebrated fifty days after Easter. Its name comes from the Greek word for "fiftieth." Originally Pentecost was a Hebrew agricultural celebration known as the Feast of Weeks. Christians see it as the birthday of the Church (see Acts 2:1-41). It's a feast that centers on the Holy Spirit, promised by Jesus. Since the tenth century, the Liturgy of the Hours—those prayers said throughout the day—for Pentecost has included a ninth-century hymn, "Veni Creator Spiritus"—Come Creator Spirit.

Ordinary Time, II

After Pentecost, the Church returns to Ordinary Time but it does include a few Sundays with specific names. The first, one week after Pentecost, is Holy Trinity. The next is Corpus Christi, or the Body of Christ.

Then, for the next several months, Sundays just have a number "in Ordinary Time" until the final Sunday of the year, the feast of Christ the King. Then it's time, once again, for the First Sunday of Advent.

Holy Days of Obligation

The Church says a part of following the third commandment ("remember to keep holy the Lord's day") means attending Mass on Sunday.

Why? Because Christ told his followers to gather for the breaking of the bread and "do this in memory of me."

The Code of Canon Law—a collection of the Church's regulations—says Sunday is "the day on which the paschal mystery is celebrated in light of the apostolic tradition." It's the day Jesus rose from the dead and, since the time of the apostles, it has been the day on which Christians meet for the Lord's Supper.

The code goes on to say that Sunday "is to be observed as the foremost day of obligation in the universal Church."

In other words, a Catholic should have a serious reason for not attending Sunday Mass.

But Sunday isn't the only day on which we're expected to join together for the Eucharist. Worldwide, there are ten other "holy days of obligation" throughout the year:

Christmas . . . . December 25
Solemnity of Mary . . . . January 1
Epiphany . . . . January 6
Feast of St. Joseph . . . . March 19
Ascension . . . . forty days after Easter
Corpus Christi . . . . Thursday after Trinity Sunday
Feast of Sts. Peter and Paul . . . . June 29
Assumption (of Mary into heaven) . . . August 15
All Saints' Day . . . . November 1
Immaculate Conception of Mary . . . December 8

But that's *worldwide*. All ten might not be on the list locally because a conference of bishops can—to quote canon law again—"abolish certain holy days of obligation or transfer them to a Sunday with the prior approval of the Holy See." (The "Holy See" means the Vatican.)

The American bishops have moved three and cut two. Epiphany, Ascension and Corpus Christi are celebrated on the nearest Sunday. And the feasts of St. Joseph and Sts. Peter and Paul are off the list.

The U.S. bishops made another adjustment, too. Since 1993, Catholics aren't obligated to attend Mass on the Solemnity of Mary, the Assumption or All Saints' Day when that feast falls on a Saturday or a Monday.

Weekday Masses

So far we've talked only about Sundays and holy days of obligation. But what about regular days? What about weekdays that aren't holy days?

On the liturgical calendar, weekday Masses are divided into several categories honoring a saint or Mary or commemorating an event in the life of Christ or the Church.

While every day is the feast of someone or something, not every feast is celebrated everywhere. (What would a "something" be? The dedication of a church in Rome, for example.)

Some feasts are on what's called the universal calendar. St. Francis of Assisi is on the universal calendar. Others are on the local calendar. St. Elizabeth Ann Seton, the first native-born American saint, would be on the calendar used in the United States.

Saints and blesseds, those one step away from sainthood, are placed on the calendar as part of the canonization process. In the early Church, being on that list meant being considered a saint.

But some weekday Masses don't focus on a saint, Mary or an event. If it isn't a prominent feast—whether local or universal—then the celebrant can choose to use the Mass from the previous Sunday, an optional memorial, a votive Mass (*Go to: "What's a Votive Mass?"*) or a Mass for the dead.

Weekday Masses during Advent and Lent are a special category. Particular prayers and readings are used for daily Mass during those seasons.

Q. & A.: Who Filled the Church's Calendar?

Did the Church always have a liturgical calendar?
No. Early Christians gathered for the Lord's Supper on the Lord's Day. The idea of a daily celebration hadn't developed yet.

Why on Sunday?
That became the day for worshiping God in the breaking of the bread because that was the day on which Jesus rose from the dead.

So what was the first date on the Church's calendar?
The great feast of that early period, the focal point and only annual commemoration, was Easter. If every Sunday was a little Easter, then there was no way "big Easter" was going to be overlooked.

Why is Easter called Easter?
According to historian St. Bede (d. 735), it comes from "Eastre," the goddess of spring. Other historians have said it comes from a mistranslation into the High German of the word for "dawn," when Jesus was seen by the women coming to anoint his body.

Why isn't it the same day every year?
It is. And it isn't. In the early Church, it was always the first Sunday after the fourteenth of Nisan, the day and month of Passover.

In the second century, a group of Christians in Asia Minor began celebrating it on Passover. Rome said those folks were wrong but they continued on their own schedule until the group fizzled out in the fifth century.

But the fourteenth of Nisan was determined by the lunar calendar, and by the third century most Christians were using the Julian solar calendar. A number of multi-year cycles were suggested in Rome and Alexandria (at that time the center of the Church in the East) and at the Councils of Arles (314) and Nicaea (325).

Nicaea is credited with declaring Easter would be on the first Sunday after the first full moon following the vernal equinox (the beginning of spring). By the eighth century, most of the Church agreed with that plan.

The last controversy—in the West—was with the Irish monks in England. They followed the Celtic calendar, and St. Augustine of Canterbury, who arrived in England in 597, used the Roman one. Over time, Rome won out and by the ninth century Easter was celebrated on the same day throughout the West.

But not the East. Eastern Churches continue to use the Sunday after Passover which may or may not be the same day used in the West.

So how did the rest of the calendar get filled?

Over time, other events associated with that central day began to be grouped around it, first mostly in Jerusalem and the Holy Land.

What events?

Palm Sunday (or Passion Sunday), the day of Jesus' triumphal entry into the city just five days before his execution. Holy Thursday, the day on which he instituted the Eucharist and on which he was betrayed and handed over to the authorities. Good Friday, the day of his death. Ascension, the day on which he ascended into heaven. And Pentecost, when the Holy Spirit came to the room in which the apostles were hiding; the "birthday" of the Church.

That was the beginning. The start of the Easter cycle of feasts.

Then what?

Christmas was the second season.

Why is Christmas on December 25?

By the sixth century, Christmas—the Mass of Christ—was celebrated almost universally on December 25.

The evangelists don't give us the date. In the third century, Clement of Alexandria suggested May 20. But the Philocalian Calendar representing Roman practices for the year 366 has "12/25" for the holy day.

Some historians speculate December 25 was chosen so it could replace the pagan winter festival to the Unconquered Sun. It occurs soon after the shortest day of the year—in the northern hemisphere—when the sun, though apparently beaten, has once again begun to make a comeback.

How did the saints get on the calendar?

At the same time—again over centuries, saints' feasts were being added and so were days honoring Mary.

Members of the early Church developed the practice of praying at the graves of their saints, the martyrs. It became customary to gather at the site on the anniversary of a saint's death and to celebrate the Eucharist there.

This wasn't the pope saying "today is the feast of St. So-and-so." It was the local bishop and the people—those who had known So-and-so, those who lived in the same area he or she was from—who did this spontaneously.

In fact, to be a canonized saint now means being listed on the Church's calendar. To have a special day in your honor. (*Go to: "A Saint Sampler."*)

Vestments and Their Colors

At the time priests first started wearing vestments for Mass, those were the common formal clothes among the Romans. Obviously, styles changed but the celebrants continued to wear the same items because, over time, each became symbolic of the priestly role.

Now Mass vestments include the:

Alb: A white tunic that goes to the ankles.

Amice: A rectangular cloth worn around the neck, tucked into the collar and going over the shoulders. Used when the alb doesn't completely cover the ordinary clothing at the neck.

Chasuble: Large poncho-like cloak.

Cincture: Cord used as a belt to tie the alb close to the body.

Stole: Long band of cloth going around the neck and falling to about the knees. A deacon wears a stole over the left shoulder, crossed and fastened on the right side.

The minimum Mass vestments for a main celebrant would be the alb, stole and chasuble. A priest who is not the main celebrant at Mass normally would wear an alb and stole.

The stole and chasuble are colored according to the particular celebration and time of year.

Green: Ordinary Time, symbol of hope and the vitality of life in the faith.

Violet: Advent and Lent, symbol of penance.

Red: Passion Sunday, Good Friday, Pentecost, feasts of apostles, evangelists and martyrs. Symbol of giving one's life for the love of God.

Rose: May be used on third Sunday of Advent and fourth Sunday of Lent. Symbol of upcoming joy during time of penance.

White: Seasons of Christmas and Easter, feasts and com-memorations of Jesus (except those of the Passion), feasts and commemorations of Mary, angels, saints who aren't martyrs, All Saints, John the Baptist, John the Evangelist, Chair of Peter and Conversion of Paul. Symbol of purity and integrity of life of faith. It may, generally, be substituted for other colors and can be used for funerals and Masses for the dead. (Black or violet could also be used for those.)

On special occasions, special vestments (fancier ones) can be worn, even if their color doesn't match the requirement for that day. For example, some parishes have gold vestments for big feast days.

Think Fast

Fasting means to cu back or go without food and drink for a religious purpose. Christians—or Jews—certainly didn't invent it, although it has long been a part of both religions.

In the Catholic tradition, fasting now applies to a couple of days each year and to preparing to receive Holy Communion.

The regulation in the United States says any Catholic between eighteen and fifty-nine is "obliged" to fast on Ash Wednesday and Good Friday. A person is allowed one full meal each day and two smaller meals. The two smaller ones shouldn't add up to more than the bigger one. Drinking ordinary liquids doesn't break the fast.

("Break the fast." Sound almost familiar? Yes, "breakfast" comes from breaking one's fast, after Mass and Communion, with the first meal of the day.)

On Ash Wednesday and all the Fridays of Lent and Good Friday, Catholics from age fourteen are not allowed to eat meat.

In the not-too-distant past, up until Vatican II, every day of Lent except Sundays was a fast day. And all Fridays of the entire year were days of abstinence from meat, except if that day was a solemnity like Christmas.

Why Friday and why the change? Friday was the day on which Jesus died. And the change wasn't because meatless Fridays or fasting daily during Lent were bad ideas, it was the Church saying it would be better if people did these things voluntarily or, in their place, chose a different form of self-denial.

What's a Votive Mass?

Votive comes from the Latin *votum* meaning a solemn vow made to a god or an offering—a donation—made for a prayer answered. It can mean a prayer or a wish.

A votive candle—often kept in a rack before an image of Jesus, Mary or a saint—is one lit by a petitioner with a prayer for a particular intention.

Votive Masses are Masses for special occasions or in honor of particular aspects of the mystery of God or the saints.

As the sacramentary, the book of liturgical prayers, explains, these are divided into three groups: ritual Masses for the celebration of certain sacraments; various needs and occasions; and Masses "of the Mysteries of the Lord or in honor of Mary or a particular saint or of all the saints," such as the Masses for the Holy Trinity, Holy Cross or Holy Name of Jesus.

A celebrant can use the text from a votive Mass when no other solemnity, feast or memorial occurs on that day.

Unfortunately, that message was pretty much lost.

Fasting also applies to Holy Communion. Before the pontificate of Pius XII, who died in 1958, a person was not allowed food or drink from midnight until Communion. During Pius XII's reign that changed. Water was allowed and it was three hours for food and one hour for drink. Since Vatican II, it has been one hour for both.

The exception is people who are elderly, ill or infirm. They, and their caregivers, can receive the Eucharist even if they haven't abstained for an hour.

A Saint Sampler

Who's on the calendar? These are some examples:

January

4. . . . . Elizabeth Ann Seton, America's first native-born saint

24. . . . . Francis de Sales, patron of Catholic writers

28 . . . . Thomas Aquinas, Dominican theologian

31 . . . . John Bosco, worked with youth in Turin, Italy

February

3 . . . . Blaise, throats are blessed on his feast day

6. . . . . Paul Miki and Companions, Japanese martyrs

10 . . . . Scholastica, the sister of St. Benedict

March

17. . . . . Patrick, patron of Ireland

April

25 . . . . Mark, evangelist

29 . . . . Catherine of Siena, mystic and doctor of the church

May

26 . . . . Philip Neri, Italian priest

27 . . . . Augustine of Canterbury, missionary to England

June

13 . . . . Anthony of Padua, patron of finding lost objects

22 . . . . Thomas More, English chancellor

29 . . . . Sts. Peter and Paul, apostles

July

22 . . . . Mary Magdalene, "apostle to the apostles"

25 . . . . James, apostle

26 . . . . Joachim and Anne, parents of Mary

31 . . . . Ignatius Loyola, founder of Society of Jesus

August

8 . . . . Dominic, founder of the Order of Preachers

11 . . . . Clare of Assisi, foundress of Poor Clares

14 . . . . Maximilian Kolbe, Auschwitz martyr

27 . . . . Monica, mother of Augustine

28 . . . . Augustine, doctor of the Church

September

27 . . . . Vincent de Paul, French priest, founder

30 . . . . Jerome, translator of Bible into Latin

October

1.............. Thérèse of Lisieux, patroness of foreign missions
4..................... Francis of Assisi, founder of Friars Minor
19... Isaac Jogues, John de Brebeuf and companions, Jesuit martyrs
28................................... Simon and Jude, apostles

November

1... All Saints
3................... Martin de Porres, Peruvian wonder worker
4.......................... Charles Borromeo, Italian cardinal
13........................... Frances Xavier Cabrini, missionary
16................................ Margaret of Scotland, queen
30.. Andrew, apostle

December

6.. Nicholas, bishop
26...................................... Stephen, first martyr
27..................................... John, evangelist apostle
28.................. Holy Innocents, young boys killed by Herod

CHAPTER EIGHT

Going Beyond Those Sixty Minutes

Life would be much easier for us Catholics if our religion was limited to that one hour at Mass on Sunday. And, for the devout, even a few half-hour weekday Masses, too.

But we know loving God involves more than presenting ourselves at the altar. After all, at the end of each Mass, we are sent.

But sent where? To do what?

In this chapter we'll look at two prominent and basic sources that talk about that. The first is one of the documents of the Second Vatican Council. The second is the *Catechism of the Catholic Church*.

The Light of All Nations

The vast majority of the world's one billion-plus Catholics are neither ordained nor professed religious. Most are lay people. The central document of Vatican II is a good place to begin examining what the Mass means—or can mean—for them.

"The Dogmatic Constitution on the Church" was issued in 1964. Sometimes it's referred to by its Latin name, *"Lumen Gentium."* That comes from its first sentence: "Christ is the light [*lumen*] of nations [*gentium*]."

Bare bones, it says not just the ordained and professed religious, but the laity, too, have an obligation to witness, to minister and to offer fellowship. Those terms are used in the New Testament.

"Really partaking of the body of the Lord in the breaking of the Eucharistic bread," the document says, "we are taken up into communion with Him and with one another"(*Lumen Gentium,* 7).

The Mass, the Eucharist, isn't just Jesus and me, singular. Yes, it's one-on-one; yes, it's personal; but it's also communal. And always has been. It is praying with and for one another.

But that doesn't mean everyone at Mass is the same. That we're programmed to go out from the Mass and live our Catholic lives in exactly the same way. Rather, our vocation, our calling from God and our being called to God, is unique.

"'Because the bread is one,'" the bishops continue, quoting from the New Testament, "'we [members of the Church] though many, are one body, all of us who partake of the one bread' (1 Cor 10:17). In this way all of us are made members of His body (cf. 1 Cor 12:27), 'but severally members one of another' (Rom 12:5)" (*Lumen Gentium,* 7).

Another translation of that last passage reads: "We belong to one another." In other words, we belong to Christ but we also depend on one another. We have a responsibility to one another.

"As all the members of the human body, though they are many, form one body [the eyes, the ears, the hands and so on], so also are the faithful of Christ (cf. 1 Cor 12:12). Also, in the building up of Christ's body various members and functions have their part to play. There is only one Spirit who, according to His own richness and the needs of the ministries, gives His different gifts for the welfare of the Church (cf. 1 Cor 12:1-11)" (*Lumen Gentium,* 7).

At the Mass, we come as different people with different needs and different obligations but through the Mass we're joined not just with Christ but with and to one another. And that connection, that interdependence with each other—and all humanity—doesn't end when Mass concludes.

Our Common Priesthood

But there's more to it than that. All of us, ordained and non-ordained Christians, share a common priesthood by virtue of our baptism. Yes, there is a distinction between the priest and the people, but the two aren't opposites. That's because all those who are baptized share in Christ's priesthood. Here's what the bishops taught in *Lumen Gentium:*

> Though they differ from one another in essence and not only in degree, the common priesthood of the faithful and the ministerial or hierarchical priesthood are nonetheless interrelated: each of them in its own special way is a participation in the one priesthood of Christ.
>
> The ministerial priest, by the sacred power he enjoys, teaches and rules the priestly people; acting in the person of Christ, he makes present the Eucharistic Sacrifice [the Mass], and offers it to God in the name of all the people. But the faithful, in virtue of their royal priesthood, join in the offering of the Eucharist. They likewise exercise that priesthood in receiving the sacraments, in prayer and thanksgiving, in the witness of a holy life, and by self-denial and active charity (*Lumen Gentium,* 10).

The document continues: "Taking part in the Eucharistic Sacrifice, which is the fount and apex [the highest point] of the whole Christian life, they offer the divine Victim to God, and offer themselves along with It. Thus, both by reason of the offering and through Holy Communion, all take part in this liturgical service, not indeed, all in the same way but each in that way which is proper to himself.

"Strengthened in Holy Communion by the Body of Christ, they then manifest in a concrete way that unity of the People of God, which is suitably signified and wondrously brought about by this most august sacrament" (*Lumen Gentium*, 11).

Through the Mass, through Communion, we *are* made one in Christ. But how I pray at Mass—what I pray about, what I offer—will be different from how you pray. And where I go after Mass—where I take that grace and how I use it in my daily life—will be different, too.

We all pray together. We're all sent. But, most often, we're sent our separate ways. "Through their Baptism and Confirmation," the document notes, "all are commissioned to that apostolate by the Lord Himself. [We're all obliged to help others learn about Christ through our words and our actions.] Moreover, by the sacraments, especially the Holy Eucharist, that charity toward God and man which is the soul of the apostolate is communicated and nourished" (*Lumen Gentium*, 33).

Through the sacraments and especially the Mass, we ourselves experience God's love in a particular way and that love grows stronger and blossoms. That maturing is stunted without a corresponding love for others. If I don't love my neighbor I can't claim to love God. Jesus, after all, was very blunt about that. When we feed the hungry, visit the sick and so on, we are doing that to him (see Mt 25:31-46). We'll be judged on that.

But, again, the differences within that unity have to be considered. I can't compare what I do—what I am called to do—with what someone else does. That's because "every layman, in virtue of the very gifts bestowed upon him, is at the same time a witness and a living instrument of the mission of the Church herself, 'according to the measure of Christ's bestowal' (Eph 4:7)" (*Lumen Gentium,* 33).

So non-ordained folks aren't off the hook simply because they're non-ordained. Far from it. In fact, "the laity, dedicated to Christ and anointed by the Holy Spirit, are marvelously called and wonderfully prepared so that ever more abundant fruits of the Spirit may be produced in them. For all their works, prayers, and apostolic endeavors, their ordinary married and family life, their daily occupations, their physical and mental relaxation, if carried out in the Spirit, and even the hardships of life, if patiently borne—all these become 'spiritual sacrifices acceptable to God through Jesus Christ' (cf. 1 Pt 2:5). Together with the offering of the Lord's body, they are most fittingly offered in the celebration of the Eucharist. Thus, as those everywhere who adore in holy activity, the laity consecrate the world itself to God" (*Lumen Gentium,* 34).

Let's take a closer look at that last paragraph because there's an awful lot in it.

If you are a lay person, you are:

- Dedicated to Christ.
- Anointed by the Holy Spirit.
- "Marvelously called" and able to have increased within you the fruits of the Holy Spirit. What are those "fruits"? Traditionally, they're listed as love, joy, peace, patience, kindness, goodness, faith, gentleness and self-control. It isn't that you produce them out of nothing, but seek them and

nurture them, allowing the Spirit to shape your behavior.

- Everything you do—everything—can be offered to God. Not just your prayers and obvious acts of charity, but your ordinary, everyday family life and all it entails. Your work, no matter what it may be. The things you do for fun. Your heartaches and pain. All of it can be offered to God at Mass.
- When you do this, when you take your entire life—lived in the world—you are offering the world to God.

Living in the World

The document doesn't beat around the bush when it comes to describing the role lay people are called to play: "They are in their own way made sharers in the priestly, prophetic and kingly functions of Christ" (*Lumen Gentium,* 31).

Christ, who offered himself to the Father on Calvary. Who offers himself, and is offered, at each Mass.

The Mass is, or can become, the core, the foundation, the springboard, for a layman or laywomen. But lay people aren't supposed to be cloistered in a church building. Or think of their Christian call as limited to attending Mass.

According to *Lumen Gentium,*

The laity, by their very vocation, seek the kingdom of God by engaging in temporal affairs and by ordering them according to the plan of God. They live in the world, that is, in each and in all of the secular professions and occupations. They live in the ordinary circumstances of family and social life, from which the very web of their existence is woven.

They are called there by God so that by exercising their

proper function and led by the spirit of the Gospel they may work for the sanctification of the world from within as a leaven. In this way they can make Christ known to others, especially by the testimony of a life resplendent in faith, hope and charity (*Lumen Gentium,* 31).

Leaven. Now there's a biblical image. The yeast that transforms. The bishops use another New Testament word, too. "The laity are called in a special way to make the Church present and operative in those places and circumstances where only through them can it become the salt of the earth" (*Lumen Gentium,* 33).

How is that done? "The laity go forth as powerful proclaimers of a faith in things to be hoped for (cf. Heb 11:1), when they courageously join to their professions of faith a life springing from faith" (*Lumen Gentium,* 35).

They walk their talk.

"This evangelization, that is, this announcing of Christ by a living testimony as well as by the spoken word, takes on a specific quality and a special force in that it is carried out in the ordinary surroundings of the world" (*Lumen Gentium,* 35).

Sent from Mass into the ordinary world, the Catholic layperson can show others what it means to believe in Jesus by what she does, by how he lives his life. Most often, that impact comes not from preaching, but from example.

Why is she so kind to others? Why does he have that sense of peace?

Sent from Mass into the ordinary world, the Catholic layperson touches lives in a way that a nun or a priest, a bishop or even the pope can't. Others see that layperson and know that, in most ways, she's just like them. But she's different, too. In a good way. Why? What's her secret?

It isn't a secret. Or shouldn't be. A Catholic knows he is loved by God. And he strives to become better at loving God. And as he does that—as he becomes, truly, more "God-like"— he acts as that leaven. He is that salt.

Just as the Mass has the power to touch him, to transform him, he is sent from that celebration to touch and transform the lives of others. It's an obligation, not an option. It's part of every Catholic's vocation. To be that leaven, that salt, in a particular home, a particular family, a particular neighborhood, school and workplace.

With fellow Christians, "by their combined efforts [to] remedy the customs and conditions in the world, if they are an inducement to sin, so that they all may be conformed to the norms of justice and may favor the practice of virtue rather than hinder it" (*Lumen Gentium*, 36).

"By so doing," the document points out, laypeople "will imbue [penetrate and permeate] culture and human activity with moral values" (*Lumen Gentium*, 36).

We are sent to change the world, in so many ways. A seemingly impossible task for a human alone. A worthy challenge— a calling, a true possibility—for a human relying on God's help and centering his or her life on God's love.

In the Catechism

Now let's look at another source.

The *Catechism of the Catholic Church* doesn't use the exact words from the 1980 movie "The Blues Brothers" but that's its meaning: We're on a mission from God.

Really.

"Mission—a requirement of the Church's catholicity" reads a subhead in the *Catechism* (*CCC* 849). It's a mandate. A basic command. "'Having been divinely sent to the nations that she might be "the universal sacrament of salvation," the Church, in obedience to the command of her founder and because it is demanded by her own essential universality, strives to preach the Gospel to all men': 'Go therefore and make disciples of all nations, baptizing them in the name of the Father and of the Son and of the Holy Spirit, teaching them to observe all that I have commanded you; and Lo, I am with you always, until the close of the age.'"[10]

Why does God give us this mission? The same reason he sent his Son. He loves us. He wants us—all humans—to be with him forever. And the way is Jesus.

The *Catechism* notes that among the many terms used for the Eucharistic celebration (Lord's Supper, breaking of the bread, holy sacrifice and others) is "Holy Mass (*Missa*), because the liturgy in which the mystery of salvation is accomplished" (*CCC* 1332) ends with the sending forth (*missio*) of the people, so that they can go and fulfill God's will in their daily lives.

It's God's will for us, his plan, that we are sent to tell others about Jesus—through our words, our deeds, our lifestyle. That doesn't mean we get a bullhorn and announce "Look at me! Look at me! Look at me!"

It means, to use an image from one of Christ's parables, that we are the light set on a lamp stand, not put under a bushel basket (see Mt 5:14-16). We are the city on the mountain. We can be seen. We are "the light of the world." And we have to shine so that others see what we have and what we do and are drawn to the Father.

At times it's tempting to think conversion is a numbers game. Catholics are one team and if we get more members, then we're winning. But our mission isn't about adding to the roster for the roster's sake.

It's about easing people's pains now. Lessening their fears now. And helping them share eternity with God, face to face, later.

We are sent from the Mass because at the Mass, in the Mass, we find the truth. "I am the way, and the truth, and the life," Jesus said (Jn 14:6). Everyone wants the truth. It tells us what's important and what isn't. It tells us why we were created. It allows us to make choices that lead us to joy now and eternal happiness later.

Life is still hard, even if we know the truth. There is still pain and sickness and death. But if we know the truth, we don't have to flounder through life. We can know that in spite of pain and sickness and death, we were created by Love. Love has not abandoned us. And one day we can all be united in Love forever.

We're on a mission because God knows nothing else satisfies the human heart like he does. Nothing else makes sense the way he does. And, as Christians, we know the way to the Father is through Jesus. We know that because Jesus told us. Right after he said he was the way, the truth and the life.

Again, this doesn't mean our family, friends, neighbors and coworkers want to be preached to. Perhaps there might be an appropriate time to say a word or two about our beliefs. But, generally, it is our very life—our being the city on the hill, the light on the lamp stand—that may first catch their attention. That may lead them to question, in their own hearts, what we have that they don't. That may move them to open the discussion on these things. That may help them notice something is lacking in their lives but not in ours.

They may spot those fruits of the Holy Spirit and want them for themselves. (Who doesn't want more joy, peace, patience and the others?) What's our secret? Being sent from the Mass means there is no secret. This information—this Truth, with a capital T—is available for anyone.

Is *for* everyone.

The Mass isn't a closed-door ritual that's part of an exclusive club. It's the foundation and the source for a lifestyle that's meant for all of us. We're supposed to be living invitations, pointing the way, welcoming, others who are looking for the Truth.

And, the *Catechism* notes, it places another obligation on us, too.

We have the Mass because Jesus loved his apostles. Because he loves us. Because he loves, in a particular way, the poor.

"The Lord, having loved those who were his own, loved them to the end. Knowing that the hour had come to leave this world and return to the Father, in the course of a meal he washed their feet and gave them the commandment to love (Jn 6:68)" (*CCC* 1337).

We Catholics are called to serve others.

"In order to leave them a pledge of his love, in order never to depart from his own and to make them sharers in his Passover, he instituted the Eucharist" (*CCC* 1337).

And "the Eucharist commits us to the poor. To receive in truth the Body and Blood of Christ given up for us, we must recognize Christ in the poorest" (*CCC* 1397).

At the end of each Mass, we're sent to serve the most needy. How and where we do that will vary from person to person. But the why is clear. It is what Christ did. It's what's commanded us to do.

And, Jesus tells us, it's where we'll continue to find him.

During those sixty minutes at Mass, we can receive him, his Body and his Blood. Outside Mass, we can give back to him. We can feed him. Clothe him. Comfort him. It's the Mass that helps us recognize him outside the Mass, in what Mother Teresa once referred to as his "disturbing disguise."

"Go," the priest says. And one small word means so much.

We're sent. We're on a mission from God.

CHAPTER NINE

How to Worship at a Mass that "Fits Right"

We mean no disrespect here. Ice cream is ice cream. But it can come in a variety of flavors. The Mass is the Mass. But it can be celebrated in a variety of ways *and* you can participate in that celebration in a variety of roles.

How do you find one that best matches your needs at this particular time in your life? How do you discover the best way for you to take part in that liturgical celebration?

It takes work.

The Mass isn't supposed to be a spectator event. It's not like a play or a movie. To use a computer term, it's designed to be interactive. If we come to Mass to be entertained, we're likely to be disappointed. If we come with the expectation that we can just sit back and the Mass will somehow move us, we're likely to leave less than satisfied.

Yes, sometimes a particular parish will have a particular Mass that features a tremendous choir or outstanding musician. Yes, some churches have a priest or deacon who is a phenomenal preacher.

Yes, sometimes when we do just sit back, we are moved anyway. The Spirit, which blows where it will, stirs our soul in spite of our attitude.

But, generally speaking, the Mass is very much like the rest of our life. We will get more out of it if we put more into it.

The truth is we humans become accustomed to things very quickly. The extraordinary soon becomes ordinary. We don't marvel at open-heart surgery or cell phones anymore, for example.

And even the miraculous becomes common. This wafer of unleavened bread and this cup of wine are changed into the Body and Blood of Christ, who is God. Into the Creator and Sustainer of the universe. Every day at 8:00 A.M. and three times on Sunday morning.

In every parish, in every town, in every country throughout the world.

At every Mass we don't just witness a miracle, we take part in one. We have the opportunity to step forward and receive one. To accept, in such an intimate and personal way, the Creator into our bodies and into our souls.

And, soon, it becomes very ordinary unless we work at keeping it fresh. Keeping it vibrant. Keeping it moving to deeper levels.

In a way, Mass is like a meal shared by a longtime married couple. God is always ready to open our minds, touch our hearts, help us shoulder our daily crosses. But, at times, we choose to be the spouse who keeps his nose buried in the newspaper at breakfast. Who keeps her eyes glued to the television screen during dinner.

So the first step to getting more out of the Mass is one that's incredibly simple and continually challenging. To get more out of the Mass we have to want to get more out the Mass.

We have to want to deepen that relationship. We have to want to make the prayers more meaningful for us. We have to want to make receiving Jesus in the Eucharist an extraordinary event, even if it's one that happens often.

Fortunately, and certainly not surprisingly, God is on our side. God wants those things for us because he wants all good things for us. He wants us to have nothing but the very best. And that doesn't mean a newer car, snazzier clothes, a winning lottery ticket. It means being drawn closer to him, because there's nothing better than that.

There's nothing better than heaven. And heaven is spending eternity with him, face to face. Sometimes this is referred to as the beatific vision. That means seeing God is the ultimate happiness.

So we say we want the Mass to mean more and we ask God for that and then.... Then, in a sense, God puts responsibility back on us. We are dependent on God for that increase in faith, hope and love, but often it comes when we take advantage of the means he offers to make it happen.

Making It Happen

If we ask, we'll be given opportunities to begin to make it happen. Or, perhaps more accurately, we'll begin to better see the opportunities that have been there for some time.

What might some of them be?

- Free will. This is a good place to start. God has given each of us the ability to choose. To analyze and then decide. And to listen. He calls us in so many ways throughout our lifetime. He encourages us to make his will our will by helping us make choices that lead us to him.

  Not just big choices, like marriage, single life or ordained or religious life. But small ones, too. Mass is a good example.

Typically, we get to choose when and where and how we pray. When and where and how we go to Mass.

For instance, one celebration features a traditional choir and classical music. Another is designed for teens. A third may be very early in the morning. A fourth caters more to families with young children. And so on.

None of this means we'll get nothing out of a Mass that doesn't—to use crude marketing terms—have us in mind as the target. Jesus is present at every Mass. We can worship the Father at every Mass. We can be open to the Spirit at every Mass.

But if there is a particular priest who makes us grind our teeth every time he speaks, or a particular time that we're always sleepy, or a particular type of music that simply irritates us, we should try to worship at a different liturgy, if possible.

But it would be a tragedy to let that particular priest, time or music become the excuse we use to stop attending any Mass. It can help to consider that God may be offering us something special in that setting. We may *need* that priest, time or music to increase our patience, our perseverance or our charity. We may *need* that reminder that, unlike a gourmet restaurant or blockbuster movie, the Mass doesn't have to rate "five stars" to be the Mass. We may *need* those incidentals that disturb us to learn to partake more fully in the one essential that can bring us peace of mind.

Let's look at some other opportunities to make Mass mean more.

- Ministry. There are opportunities to actively participate in the Mass. To get up out of our pew and perform a service.

In the recent past, many of those were limited to males. Men could be ushers. Boys could serve. That's no longer the case. Now all children can be acolytes. And, on occasion, they can help in other ways, too, as lectors, ushers and greeters.

Adults—those who have been confirmed—can be Eucharistic ministers. Helping the celebrant distribute Holy Communion. And adults can be lectors.

All ages can sing in choirs and play instruments. All can bring up the gifts at the Preparation of Gifts.

But what if we don't want to play a special role in the liturgy? Even then, there are things we can do to make the Mass more present to us. Or us more present at the Mass.

- One is spend some time preparing. Check out what the Sunday readings are going to be and go over them ahead of time. How do we know what's coming? Look in the missalette (the booklet used in many parishes) for next Sunday's selection or, during the week, go online to find them.

  Not sure what a reading means? There are a number of fine books available that can help there. The parish priest or director of religious education can make suggestions.

  Even a familiar passage may have new meaning for us depending on what we're experiencing in our own life at that particular time. A good example is the story of the Prodigal Son (see Lk 15:11-32). Sometimes we may identify with the spendthrift son, sometimes with the dutiful lad who stayed home, sometimes with the forgiving father.

- Get to the celebration ahead of time. Allow a few minutes to pray before the Mass begins. Most of us have to stop and take a breath before we can more fully turn our attention to God in prayer.

- See ourselves as "ministers of hospitality," recognizing and greeting the presence of Christ in others as the congregation comes together.

- Don't be discouraged if our attention strays. Even during the Mass itself. Sometimes, rather than fighting that urge to think about other concerns, it's better to bring those concerns into focus and present them to God. This is what I'm worried about, Lord. This is what scares me. This is what I'm unsure of.

   At some Masses, that will be our main offering. And, from a parent's point of view, it's not a bad one. Any mom or dad would like a child coming to him or her and voicing concerns. Asking for help. Looking for guidance. Our loving Father is no different. That shouldn't be surprising. After all, he created us in his image.

- Pray the prayers being offered during the Mass. Listen to the words. Give the responses. The liturgy is less likely to feel like a "rerun" if we do more than put our body in the pew. If, instead, we also put our heart and mind into the celebration.

- On the other hand, realize sometimes the liturgy may not touch us on an emotional level. That doesn't make it less valid or valuable. And if we pursue only an emotional lift we may be missing out on what else is being offered to us. We may overlook or ignore what gift the Spirit is presenting to us, a gift that we may need, right then, more than feeling good.

- Sing the songs. Traditionally, this is one area where Catholics haven't shined. On the other hand, it's been said singing is praying twice. The bishops at Vatican II were very clear, calling all Catholics to full, active and conscious participation in the liturgy. This includes those with less than stellar singing voices.

- Go to Holy Communion. This has become more common in recent times but it should never be ordinary. If we have committed a serious sin, we should go take advantage of the sacrament of reconciliation—go to confession—before receiving. In the past, some people received so infrequently, stressing their unworthiness, that the Church imposed an "Easter duty" law. Every adult was to receive at least once a year, during Easter time. This is still the case.

Now we realize that, although we're never truly worthy, God invites us to receive often. But that doesn't free us from the obligation to prepare ourselves, mentally and spiritually, for that encounter.

- Don't become discouraged if, at this point in our life, it's hard to take part in the Mass. This can be especially true if we come with our young children. It's difficult not to be distracted when we have to keep one eye, or both eyes, on them for a good part of the Mass.

  Remember it well may be that a mother's harried prayer is like the widow's mite (see Lk 21:3-4). On the surface, it doesn't seem like much compared to what others are offering. But, God knows, it's given from her substance.

- Get to know fellow parishioners. This can be hard in today's large parishes. But it can make a difference when we realize we're there praying with, and praying for, friends.

  Often, that relationship begins and grows outside the Mass. It takes place in other parish activities.

  One other point about large parishes: Unfortunately, Catholic churches can feel unwelcoming to newcomers. A visitor can have no one say hello except at the sign of peace. If you're a visitor, don't take this personally (although it can be hard not to). The truth is even longtime parishioners may not know other longtime parishioners. Most assume an unrecognized face belongs to a parishioner who typically attends a different Mass.

You are welcome. You do belong there. You are wanted and needed.

- Go every Sunday. Why does Catholicism say a person should attend Sunday Mass unless he has a serious reason for missing? That goes back to the book of Exodus and the commandment God gave to Moses.

The "Sabbath" Was Made for Us

What we should keep in mind is God doesn't need us to worship him. In no way is he dependent on us. Rather, the opposite is true. We humans, with our short attention spans, need to be reminded that we are dependent on him. That there is a Supreme Being whom we owe, big time. And who, by his very nature, is to be adored.

But the Sabbath wasn't created for God. Again, God doesn't need a Sabbath. We do. We need that day of rest. Sadly, in our own time, it's been all but lost and we're paying the price.

Going to Sunday Mass is a step toward recapturing what's ours. Reclaiming the basic right to, after turning to the Creator in prayer, sharing a more relaxed time with loved ones.

The better we become at developing that rhythm, that this is the day we worship together and turn the speed of life down a notch, the more we will get from the Mass and from the rest of the day, too. From our private prayer life. From the rest of the week.

Why does it matter? In some ways we can be like the consumer who buys a product and ignores the directions that come with it. Or, even more foolishly, we have access to the designer and creator of the product but we don't turn to him for help.

God designed and created us. And the world in which we live. It was *his* idea that one day a week be set aside. *His* idea that we can be with his Son in a very particular way at Mass. *His* idea that we come together and pray with and for one another as we remember—and he re-presents—the sacrifice Jesus made.

Simply on a common-sense level, it would be foolish to ignore this. And on a spiritual level, it could be sinful, meaning a turning away from God. Again, God always lets us choose. He never forces. Not only does he love us that much, but he has that much confidence in us.

The Mass is his gift to us. He invites us to this table, this altar of sacrifice. His table. The altar on which his Son was offered. And is offered.

Even after we accept that invitation we have choices. Comparing it to a party, we can be the wallflower or the one having a whee of a time on the dance floor. We can be there, bodily, because "Mom said I had to go." Or we can *really* be present.

To an outsider, it may seem that everyone attending a Mass is in lockstep. Stand, sit, kneel. Answer, sing, come forward for Communion. But that just isn't so. It's easy to go through the motions, especially if we've been doing them for years. But going through the motions isn't really the same as going to Mass.

These words aren't meant to be a scolding for folks who are less than attentive at the Eucharist. We all are at times. Rather, they're meant to emphasize something that we already know. Something that is so well known it's a cliché.

But to say it once again: We're going to get out of it what we put into it.

But that isn't completely accurate. That could be the case if we were speaking about education, for example. If we study hard, do our homework, pay attention and participate in class, it's not hard to predict what will happen. We will master that discipline at that level.

But with the Mass, there's more. With spirituality, there's more. When it comes to our relationship with God, we get more out of it than we put into it. Every time. Our God is a generous God. He gives us, to quote Jesus, a measure back that is packed down and overflowing (see Lk 6:38). Our God, to borrow an image from another parable, is a God who gives us a full day's pay even if we've only begun working late in the afternoon (see Mt 20:1-16).

Why? The same reason he created us. The same reason he stepped into human history in a particular way after we humans had messed up. The same reason he sent his very Son to save us from that mess. The same reason his Son instituted the Eucharist so we would know he has never really left us. The same reason the Father and Son sent the Spirit to give us so many gifts.

There is only one reason.

God loves us.

There is only one explanation.

God loves you.

You Are Invited

You, singular. Right here. Right now. God loves you with an infinite love. A love that had no end. A love that cannot be measured.

Right here. Right now. God invites you to turn toward him.

To take a step toward him.

Right here, right now. God repeats his standing invitation. "Join me at a meal. Sit at my table. There, I'll change bread and wine into my Body and Blood. You're welcome to eat and to drink."

The long-awaited and prayed-for Messiah, the anointed one of God, is at every Mass. The creator and sustainer of all, is at every Mass. The Spirit of love that exists between the Father and the Son, is at every Mass.

And you're on the guest list.

There's no one in the history of the world, no one in the history yet to be written, he wants there more than you. How can we say that? Because there's no one, no human being, in all creation he loves more than you.

Infinite is infinite. It can't be topped.

He created and sustains you. Singular. He became a human being and was executed and rose from the dead for you. Singular. He pours out his gifts for you. Singular.

"Lord, I am not worthy...."

None of us is. But our generous God offers all that to each of us anyway. No matter what we've done. No matter what we've failed to do. No matter how long it's been since we turned to him. Now matter how completely we've turned away or how far we've run.

No matter how much we, mistakenly, think we've gone too far or it's too late for us.

Come to my table, he says. Sit with me. Join me in the breaking of the bread, this Bread of Life.

Notes

1. *CCC* 1375, St. John Chrysostom, *prod. Jud.* 1:6:PG 49, 380.
2. *CCC* 1325, Congregation of Rites, instruction, *Eucharisticum mysterium,* 6.
3. *CCC* 1327, St. Irenaeus, *Adv. haeres.* 4, 18, 5:PG 7/1, 1028.
4. *CCC* 1323, SC 47.
5. *CCC* 1324, LG 11.
6. *CCC* 1324, PO 5.
7. *CCC* 1376, Council of Trent [1551]:DS 1642; cf. *Mt* 26:26ff; *Mk* 14:22ff; *Lk* 22:19ff; *1 Cor* 11:24ff.
8. *CCC* 1366, Council of Trent [1562]; DS 1740; cf. *1 Cor* 11:23; *Heb* 7:24, 27.
9. *CCC* 1367, Council of Trent [1562]: *Doctrina de ss. Missae sacrificio,* c.2: DS 1743; cf. *Heb* 9:14.27.
10. *CCC* 849, AG 1; cf. *Mt* 16:15; *Mt* 28:19-20.

Index

Abram, Abraham
  covenant 19
  sacrifice of Isaac 87
Adam
  creation story 12
  sons' sacrifices 88
agape 34
altar 43
altar rail 43
Arianism, Arius 38

Benedict, St.
  Rule 40
Benediction 44, 53
bishop
  in early Church 35
Blessed Sacrament
  devotion to 52-53
  Forty Hours 53

candles 43
Catechism of the Catholic Church
  mission of Catholics 128-32
Charlemagne 39
Constantine
  Edict of Milan 36
Corpus Christi
  feast 44
Council of Trent
  issues 49, 50-51
  what happened 55-58
  Mass as sacrifice 94
Counter-Reformation 50

Damasus, Pope 38
Didache 34

Easter duty 44, 139
Eucharist
  Greek for "thanksgiving" 13
  Holy Communion and Mass . . 14
  at Last Supper 14, 24-28, 34
  "breaking of the bread" 33
  under one species 43
  elevation of host 43
  How did mass get its name . 45-46
  Pope St. Pius X and age limit . . 54
  "high Mass"/"low Mass" 61
  parts of the Mass 62-81
  reception by non-Catholics . 82-83
  as sacrifice 85-96
  liturgical calendar 101-11
  vestments 115-16
  fasting 116-17
  votive Mass 117-18
  Lumen Gentium and
    mission 121-28
  Catechism of the Catholic Church
    and mission 128-32
  choosing a parish, Mass . . 133-43

Francis of Assisi, St. 40

Greek
  language of Church 38
Gregory the Great, Pope St.
  Mass reforms 38
  sacramentary 39

Hippolytus, St. 36
holy days of obligation 109-10

Isaac 20

Jacob, Israel 20
Joseph
   son of Jacob 20
   in Egypt 20
Justin Martyr, St.
   "The First Apology" 35-36
   excerpt 46

Latin
   language of Church. 38
Liturgy of the Word
   in early Church 35
liturgical movement
   Solesmes, France 54
   20th century 54-55
liturgical calendar/year 101-11
   Who filled the calendar. . . 111-14
   list of feasts 118-20
Lumen Gentium and mission . 121-28
Luther, Martin 44
   Reformation 50

Mass. . . . . see Eucharist
missal 52
Moses
   life of. 21-22

Nicene Council 39
Nicene Creed 39

Our Father
   two versions. 81-82

Passover
   Last Supper meal 19, 24-28
   first 22-24
   bread and wine at Mass . . . 33-34
Pius X, Pope St.
   Holy Communion. 54
Pius XII, Pope
   encyclicals 54
   Mass as sacrifice. 94

priest
   role at Mass. 8
   in early Church 35
Protestants
   Reformers 49
   how received name. 58-59
Reformation 49-51
   Mary. 51

sacrifice
   Luther 50
   Hebrew traditions, methods. 87-92
   in New Testament 92-94
   teaching in early Church 94
Sabbath
   Sunday as day of worship. 41
   made for humans 140-42
seder 30-31

tabernacle
   origin of 43
Temple
   What was so great about? . 97-99
transubstantiation
   What is transubstantiation? . 16-18
   Luther 50
Trinity 39

upper room
   Where was the upper room? . . 29

Vatican Council II
   vernacular 38
votive Mass
   for intention and stipend 44
   defined 117-18

Zwingli, Huldrych
   and Luther 50